Carried Away
To an Insane Asylum

Reminiscences of Growing up in an Insane Asylum in Reykjavik

Authored by

Jón Helgi

Translated and Edited by

James R. Dow

ISBN: 1478146818

ISBN 13: 9781478146810

Table of Contents

Editor and Translator's Introduction

Jón Helgi, aka Helgi Jón Schweizer, and I met about a decade ago when I was working on a manuscript his father, Bruno Schweizer, had left behind when he died in 1958. It was a massive work on the grammar of a German dialect spoken in northern Italy, Cymbrian. I was able to present him and his family with the published work on the fiftieth anniversary of his father's death, November 11, 2008. While I worked on the manuscript I found it necessary, and more importantly, highly desirable to pay repeated visits to the Schweizer family in the lovely little town of Diessen, located on a beautiful lake in Upper Bavaria, the Ammersee. They received me, and later me and my wife, with open arms. We got to know the entire family, and now keep up on family growth—new grandchildren—travels, and even house renovations. They have always been gracious hosts.

In the Spring of 2011, while on a fact finding mission for "one last" research project, I received a copy of Jón Helgi's reminiscences of growing up in crazy Iceland. I had read previous installments, but this one seemed intriguing, because of the setting, the psychiatric clinic Kleppur, in Iceland. Because I was busy for most of the trip, I just packed the small volume in my suitcase and left it there until I was finished with my work. On my last night in Berlin, after working for several days in the German Federal Archives, I needed to read something different from all of the letters and documents I had just finished working my way through, and so I sat in a nice Italian restaurant, ordered my meal and a glass of wine, and began reading. Almost immediately I started laughing, first just chuckling, but as I read on I found myself laughing out loud, to the point that I finally had to point to what I was reading so that the other guests in the restaurant didn't think *I* was crazy. On my next trip to Diessen, in the Fall of 2011, I suggested that the work should be translated and published in English. The response was most gratifying, and here, in English is the story of a young boy being "carried away: to an insane asylum" in Reykjavik, in Iceland.

There are, of course, many Icelandic and German names and phrases in the book, all of which have been either translated or explained. Thus there are some letters that need to be explained, actually very few. Umlauts abound in both languages, and represent lip rounding in pronunciation. Accents indicate emphasis in speaking. Most unusual for English speakers are the two versions of -*th*- used in Icelandic, printed in upper and lower cases as *Þ or þ* and *Ð or ð*. They represent voiced and unvoiced pronunciations of -*th*-, like *the*re (voiced) and wi*th* (unvoiced), e.g., in the phrase *Það er gaman að lifa* ("It is wonderful to live"), found in Chapter 2.

Finally we both would like to thank all the members of our families for their continuing support of our professional and our personal work, most especially our wives, Wicki Schweizer and Susan Dow. Thanks go also to Gunnar Schweizer, who was a major figure in much of the book. We dedicate our book to all of the dear people of Kleppur in Reykjavik.

JRD

Preface

Many unusual life stories were born in the confusion of the last
world war. In the year 1945 I was a six-year-old boy, half German
and half Icelander; I traveled with my mother and younger brother
on a mysterious path through the ruins of Germany, through what
had once been enemy territory, across the mine-infested North
Atlantic to Iceland, and landed in Kleppur, the psychiatric asylum
at Reykjavik. My mother, an Icelander herself and a trained nurse,
found work there, most likely because of her amazingly calming
effect on the patients. Psychoactive drugs played no meaningful
role in psychiatry at that time—emotional troubles were able to
develop unhindered.

The asylum and its inhabitants were a new world for my brother
and me, but soon became our normal, everyday, and developmen-
tal environment. Kleppur became our family home. The Icelandic
language and culture, and especially the city of Reykjavik and all
its inhabitants, were opened up to me from this unusual vantage
point. Kleppur was not so much a crazy place but a world apart. For
me the view was not at all disoriented or somehow damaged, but
actually more open and expansive than the Germany left behind.
I learned to move about in that confusing zone where abnormal-
ity and abnormal normality meet. I learned through many years of
naive and lovingly curious contacts to communicate with people

whose world is distant, in a bizarre way, from that which the healthy, the normal, see as reality.

The world of the healthy, especially that of my Catholic relatives far away in Bavaria, found this most troubling. The child, so they thought, would be negatively affected by his experience. Anyone who grows up in a crazy world, in the society of crazy people, will sooner or later also become crazy; at least that was their prevailing assumption.

Living in a boarding school, where students live and are taught, didn't turn out to be the best choice for me, but at least my religious salvation was secure. I had to transfer to a Catholic school, at the other end of the city, and I was thus not subjected to the spiritual confusion of Protestantism.

I got to know the city and its inhabitants as an interesting variant to the "normality" experienced in the asylum, and learned to make my way in this world too. I became an Icelander among Icelanders, and finally decided to become an Icelandic writer so that I could create wonderful and crazy worlds in my own head.

Then everything turned out differently for us, and my mother returned with me to where I had been transported away from, to the firm reality of Upper Bavaria. But this place proved to be only a new variant of the crazy normality that I had come to know so well.

CHAPTER ONE

War's End

No one can really comprehend war, even when one is immediately affected by it. Many are convinced that they are the only ones who know what is going on, but they actually understand war even less than those who have questions. Children who are born during a war sometimes don't ask themselves what is happening or whether there is something they can do to counter it. The peak of the catastrophe they experience is so limited that, with luck, they are able to see only the good side of what is happening all around them.

We—my parents, my brother, and I—were still living in Germany at the end of the war, in a small, nice, but uncomfortable house in Diessen am Ammersee, called the Little Water Castle. It was decorated with useless small towers and the village brook ran past it, and sometimes through it—the stream sometimes flooded in the summer.

Parental home in Diessen am Ammersee

My father, a philologist by profession, spent his time sorting though massive piles of note cards. With the help of a few women assistants, he studied the speech and customs of German-speaking villagers living in mountains far away from us. It was important for the war—so the regime said. Regardless, it kept the villagers away from him. And thus they had reason to doubt how faithful he was to the party line and how enthusiastic he felt about the war.

Anyone who didn't actually participate in the war led a dangerous life. Just one small side step, one moment of forgetfulness, or one wrong remark, and you were suspected of being the enemy. You were considered to be the enemy within, a traitor in the ranks who had to be dealt with quickly. Indeed, such people were thought more dangerous than an honorable opponent on the field of battle.

People in general try to survive a war—in whatever way they can—and naturally it is best if one is on the side of the victors. It is better not to try to put a stop to a war, even though all are waiting for it to finally come to an end. Anyone who gets in the way will be run over and flattened like a fly under a landslide. Flies don't bury themselves of their own free will, but humans do. They do it in spite of knowing better, with the typical human hope that some higher power will reward their crazy courage, or perhaps in the equally insane view that they owe it to themselves. Intelligent humans then lay out plans while activists go to the streets. The latter are quashed somewhat faster than the former. My father and his like-minded comrades were for the most part able to outlast the war. They received no rewards from anyone; on the contrary, they had been opponents of the system, and to be sure not just of that one.

At the end it was good people, the victors, whose arrival my parents had longed for. Based on the recommendations of old villains, however, my father was thrown into prison, and it was his imprisonment that laid the groundwork for my mother to set out with her two boys on a trip to her homeland, Iceland.

The horrors of the war reached Diessen in a relatively harmless and watered-down way. What we most feared was that the bomber pilots on their way to destroy Munich would drop a bomb on us by mistake, or, on their way back home, unload everything they hadn't dropped on the city. Every time the siren on the roof of city hall sounded (which happened more and more often toward the end of the war) the citizens of Diessen would retreat into their beer cellars. If it was nighttime, my father would always find time, while escorting me to the cellar of a neighbor's house, to point out the various lights on the airplanes up in the sky.

During these dangerous times, dark figures crept around our house at night, and on one occasion one of them fell and broke a window. It wasn't until much later that I understood it was Icelandic students living with my parents. When they listened to the radio, they turned the volume down so low that they had to put their ears right up to the loudspeaker to be able to understand anything at all.

The times were difficult, uncomfortable, and full of privations, but you don't really notice this if you don't know otherwise. A child can make only limited comparisons. We spent hours walking through the woods, pulling a wagon to pick up pieces of wood and pinecones for heating. The forests were a long way off, and had already been gleaned of undergrowth. For grown-ups that seemed burdensome, but for children it was an exciting trip into the woods. Ice on the kitchen floor was horrible for a housewife, but for children it was a wonderful opportunity to slide and skate around. The only time I realized how hard the times really were, was the last wartime Christmas, when I found all my old toys carefully repaired by my father. The highly anticipated gifts were there, but they were surprisingly different from all the other times.

There was a lot of talk when the war was ending and the victors came to Diessen, one after the other. There were several who claimed to be our conquerors. I sat out in my grandmother's front yard and looked on with fascination at the various troop movements. In more peaceful times I had sat out there and watched the carnival or Corpus Christi processions, but this was quite a parade of different types of people, and every troop had its special national character. They marched in different ways, or not at all, had different kinds of vehicles, various kinds of uniforms, an array of skin colors, and unusual style preferences, such as wearing a lot of wristwatches.

For a long time I was not able to enjoy the spectacle, for there were just too many things happening. First, some armed and shady figures came into our house looking for watches, cameras, gramophones, and young women. Later those with eyeglasses came in and took the typewriter away and looked over the books in our library. Finally, my father also disappeared.

Up until that point, Iceland was known only as the distant homeland of my mother and the students who had been living with us, all of whom were just waiting for the day when they could go back home. The war was scarcely over when a large limousine arrived, with a very obvious Icelandic flag on it, filled with dignified-looking men in unusual uniforms looking for Icelanders who had survived the war. I recognized the Icelandic flag because my mother had always decorated our Christmas trees with flag garlands. Only later did I realize that the unusual uniforms were a kind of disguise costume, since all victors wore uniforms and the Icelanders did not have any military clothing.

Summer came and with it the Americans who politely took all of the boats and the lake for themselves, for their recuperation after the war. The Americans set up camps in the surrounding meadows and stored their food supplies there. They were very interesting, and unusual, with their laid-back behavior. The times had changed, that was abundantly clear. In general it was for the best, but not especially for us, because our father had disappeared into a prison where individuals were being interrogated. These investigations did not reveal anything suspicious in his case, but he was not released, because it seemed very suspicious that nothing could be found. The first to be released were the real evil-doers, because they were sorely needed in important offices and bureaus and also because there was a total lack of clarity about German citizens' behavior during the war.

In the summer we received numerous letters from Iceland: letters with strange stamps (without the head of the Führer) and decorated with various postmarks and with tape wrapped around them. Friends and relatives in Iceland put pressure on my mother to return home with her two boys, back to the bosom of the family.

Prospects for us in Diessen were anything but rosy (with an unsuspicious father suspiciously far away), and provisions for feeding us were anything but sufficient. And so my parents decided that my mother should take the two boys with her, to her homeland in Iceland.

Travel at the time was something of a political issue: transportation was assigned to the military and carried out with military vehicles, from one camp to the next one. Our first goal was Munich, where we stayed for several weeks.

It was summer, warm, and there was food to eat. There were lots of bomb craters to play in, and military garbage was everywhere. The actual trip to Iceland came next, and consisted of seemingly similar stages: sitting close together so that we couldn't see out, bouncing around on military trucks, then enduring some kind of full-body cleansing process, and finally being assigned into stinking group quarters. This was all very unpleasant, but the worst were the trips on the trucks that never stopped for human necessities, which had to be performed over the rear tailgate. It was both an undignified and dangerous undertaking on the potholed roads! While taking care of my business it was easy to have a look at Germany, but that was no repayment for the indignity being suffered. There wasn't much to see other than war damage. In my childish mind a thought developed, that destruction brings monotony and boredom. The more destroyed the houses were, the more the ruins resembled each other.

Underway to Iceland

Finally, after many camps and even more bone-rattling and endless truck rides, we reached the border with Denmark, and I experienced for the very first time that most pronounced need for cleanliness among Scandinavians. This time there was nothing halfway about it; we were subjected to a full-body scrubbing for disinfestation: no louse and no flea should escape from Germany. Imprinted on my mind to this day is the image of powdered and naked women, and the smell of DDT in a large barrack. That was my experience at the border.

From there we traveled by train, and the next stopping place was Copenhagen, but my brother and I could see it only by looking out the window. Danes did not think much of Germans, and the two of us spoke only German. To help us pass the time, my mother had bought us two little wooden trucks to play with.

Finally this house arrest came to an end, and we traveled on to Göteborg, where a ship was waiting for us, one that would take us on to Iceland. I didn't really anticipate much; the journey was nothing to be happy about—especially the sea voyage—nor was even our eventual goal, Iceland. The only thing that seemed worth looking forward to was the end of the trip. Because I had never been able to envision an ocean voyage, I felt like the difficulties of the trip were over when we on boarded the giant steel stern of the ship.

This metal giant was actually a miserable old freighter and was being sent to Iceland probably because the ocean was still filled with mines, and its loss would have the least commercial effect. I was comforted by the fact that the ship had been loaded down with wood to burn for power, and that on the bow were the letters *MS* for *Motor-Schiff*. It was also clear that the ship was a freighter, because it had no cabins for passengers. The lack of space was made even more difficult since we were not the only passengers; there was another young mother with her little boy who joined us. Four berths for five people were at our disposal. It was a mystery to me where the crew slept.

The trip was slow and without incident—aka boring. We were all swaying on the swells where only more swells could be seen, as far as the eye could reach. Then the wooden toy trucks from

Copenhagen came out to entertain us, and did not remind us too much of the recent horrible travel on the military trucks. An unusually friendly cook carried out his duties in the galley that ran right across the ship in such a way that breakers from the side could easily wash through the kitchen and keep it clean. I soon learned, and with the permission of the cook, that changing gravity brought on by the waves let me attach the little trucks to my feet and make them into skates to roll around in the kitchen.

One morning my mother awakened me at an unusual time. There was something to see other than water and waves: an island! They were probably the Faeroe Islands. I was so excited that, years later, I tried to create this image on paper with watercolors. Soon, however, the romantic part of the ship journey was over; the weather got worse from one day to the next, and so did the passengers.

My mother took on her professional role and took care of the seasick, as the crew, including the captain, tried to keep the ship above water. Because of the stormy seas, they had no idea of our position on the North Atlantic—as we later learned. A few days later, when the bad weather let up briefly, our captain came into our sick-bay looking very troubled and whispered something to my mother. She told me later that he had said to her that there was indeed land in sight, but not where it was supposed to be if the voyage had gone according to plan, namely on the starboard side. On the port side there were steep and ragged cliffs jutting up out of the storm. The confused captain thought he must have slipped by on the east side of Iceland, because of the storm, and now had to figure out how to get away as fast as possible from the dangerous skerry coast.

My mother was able to get him to change his course, one that would have led us directly into the famous ship graveyard, the shallows on Iceland's south coast where the volcanic ash reaches far out into the ocean for several kilometers and the ships run aground long before the crew can see land.

We were most likely in the famous narrows between the Westmann Islands and Iceland. My mother thought she could make out the islands, but she was not completely sure because of the bad weather, and so we were clearly expecting the worst. In order not to lose us in case of a shipwreck, she tied herself to my brother, around his stomach, and to me around my back, then withdrew into the bunk bed to wait out whatever might come. We were lucky, and my mother was right. The right decision was to travel straight ahead. Later we learned that the coast guard was trying to contact us by radio, but the captain didn't respond because he was too ashamed to give them his position.

In the meantime the old Icelandic seaman's wisdom was shown to be true: the fear of drowning is a proven means for overcoming seasickness. For the rest of the trip I began to think about what could have happened and just how many mines we scraped by on our journey. But I thought, if you drown, then it really *doesn't* matter. This insight did not comfort me out on the ocean, and so in the final analysis I was very happy to set foot on solid ground in Reykjavik.

CHAPTER TWO

My New Home

I knew that my mother was by profession a nurse, but I didn't know at all that she had specialized in the care of the mentally ill. In retrospect it does not surprise me, for the simple reason that she made no distinction between those who were mentally ill and those who were simply ill. Looking back I can almost believe that she could not see any difference, or perhaps she chose not to see any. Apparently this basic attitude somehow colored my own thinking to such an extent that I saw the patients in the hospital we moved into as merely sick. Up to that point, I hadn't really known very many people who were sick, even though there were a lot of people who behaved abnormally after the war—at least if we consider their behavior during peaceful times as normal.

Kleppur

Compared to the accommodations that we had to put up with on our long trip over, the little room we were assigned in the attic of the hospital was downright luxurious. Just the fact that we had walls all around us, instead of dirty sheets hanging from the ceiling, made it seem that we had our own little home.

The tiny room even had a dormer, and we could see the volcano that had spewed out lava in the past, and now was where the city, and the hospital, stood. The world was amazingly calm: no rattling, no howling, no bumping, no swaying, no retching.

The entire attic level of the hospital served as accommodations for personnel, all of whom were unmarried nurses. The only men were patients and doctors, with four exceptions: the furnace man Einar, the truck driver Ásbjörn, the plumber Steini, and the carpenter Torfi. All of these men had their own territories. Only Ásbjörn, the driver of the large, black panel truck, lived on the premises, in the former doctor's house that had become too small for his family. The head doctor, whose name, Helgi, was a continuing irritation for me, and lived in a separate "Head Doctor's House."

All the nurses had small rooms in the attic, as we did, or a similarly sized room in the basement. In the middle of the attic was a common room, a kind of lounge with comfortable chairs for the employees. From there long corridors led to the left and to the right, along the roofline, to the nurses' quarters. The nurses could be identified by their uniforms, and could thus also be distinguished from the patients. Their rank was also clearly identifiable, from the apprentices who shared rooms, to the registered nurses who had their own rooms.

Mother as Nurse

The dominant color was bright white, a color that they appeared to really love, and not only for clothing. Probably, or so I thought, because it was clean-looking and fulfilled the wish to see any little stain as soon as possible, and thus be able to get rid of it. This great love of cleanliness, one might surmise, is a reaction to the mucky weather that prevailed in Iceland.

In contrast, Icelanders always have dirty shoes on their feet. In order to keep the floor in the house from looking like the dirt surrounding the house, they regularly take off their shoes and leave them at the threshold entrance. This results in a highly developed culture of cleanliness, foot hygiene, and confusion. Especially in public places, for example in a restaurant, it could be very difficult to identify one's own shoes in the mountain of footwear at the door. City dwellers had it easier than those who lived out in the country. Thanks to better streets and specialty shoe stores, the former wore a different variety of shoes, and thus didn't have the problem that country folk had with their dogs. The dogs that accompanied the farmers into town liked to lie down in the pile of shoes, to be close to their masters. In the process they made a mess of the orderly arrangement of shoes, a real necessity when you tried to find the shoes you came in with.

To understand this dilemma better, one must realize that the choice of shoes particularly, in rural areas of Iceland, was exceptionally meager, and in many cases nonexistent. To be precise, shoes were different only in size, or, in some cases (when they were made by the manufacturer), different for the left than for the right foot. It was, however, easy to distinguish shoes from boots, but the latter were considered decadent and were for pompous asses only.

The classic Icelandic shoe was made of sheepskin and looked pretty much like the moccasins made by Indians or the gym shoes worn by the founder of German gymnastics, *Turnvater* Jahn. Because of the weather conditions in Iceland, such shoes presented a clear handicap; they were only somewhat water repellant. When wet they were soft and slippery, and when on occasion they dried out, they became hard and rough. It was the automobile that brought a new and often overlooked dimension to mobility in Iceland: namely, rubber shoes. These were made from the inner tubes taken out of the tires and no longer held the air in but now kept the water out. They were universally grey-black and all had the same form that came from the curved shape of automobile tires. Among shoes they were a kind of cross-country style.

Rubber shoes

The origin of this airtight footwear made from tires led to issues that became apparent only with time, noticeably affecting the foot and the nose. It is easy to understand how this phenomenon was manifested in large restaurants, where all the guests sat airing out their socks, but it may be best not to think about all those stinky feet. Actually it is very fortunate that many of the Icelanders' favorite dishes go well with such a dominant smell. Half spoiled ray fish is in first place.

This kind of thinking did not come to me immediately on my arrival in Iceland. Instead I was inclined to see everything through rose-colored glasses, and to smell them that way too.

Christmas was approaching, and during the season in Iceland everything is both bright and dark. Dark for geographical and astronomical reasons, since the sun peeps only briefly over the horizon at midday, as if it were just looking to see if everything was still there. It was with human hands, however, that the season became bright, through an abundance of electricity. The prevailing color of the lights was of course red: bright red, with pink reflections.

Garlands were hung from the ceilings all over the hospital, almost like Bavaria was getting ready to celebrate *Fasching* (shrovetide; *mardi gras*) here. The inmates in the hospital were absolutely partial to brightly colored paper. Cotton was used to imitate cool snow in the warm interior. All during December we all thought that Christmas would come tomorrow. Happy anticipation—some say the best happiness—was masterfully celebrated.

Santa Claus, known to me from Bavaria only as St. Nicholas, came in stages in Iceland and indeed in the shape of a mischievous little rascal. I placed this creature somewhere in the half-light between the saintly figure St. Nick and his creepy companion, the *Krampus* (bogeyman).[1] As an adolescent, I noticed that these horned and ugly little Christmas creatures appeared in irregular numbers; there was one, or eight, or thirteen, or something like that. They seemed to me, when I first saw them, as an incarnation or warning of juvenile bad habits. They stole the smoked meat from the chimney, begged for candles, licked out the pots and pans, slammed the doors, gawked through the windows, and sniffed around cracks in the doors, to name just a few of their bad habits. The educational mission of the rascals (who, by the way, disappeared one by one after Christmas), would certainly have been clearer to me if I had been told that their exceptionally ugly

---

1 A *Krampus* is a demonic figure frequently associated with the gift-giver, whose role is to find out if the children have been naughty or nice during the last year. Small *Krampus* figures, made of dates and nuts, are found at the Christmas markets throughout Germany and Austria today.

mother Grýla liked to feed on children who misbehaved. Most unusual was the fact that misbehaving and lazy adults were gobbled up by a cat, one that was also part of the pre-Christmas activities. Grýla's husband, with the most unusual name of Seppaludi (*Lappenflacker* [cloth flicker]), was tied to his bed at home, suffering from laziness while she roamed about looking for something to feed him: *children.* It is difficult to describe how my mother dealt with this deeply disturbed family, and then tried to carry out her healing mission.

What I had learned about the Christmas festival back in Diessen was not immediately apparent here. The closest thing was the paper churches, carefully made from scraps of paper. Snow made of cotton covered the roof of the mini-churches, and the windows were covered with yellow cellophane paper. They glowed with such Christmas red that we had the feeling the fire trucks would arrive at any moment.

A lot of paper hung on the tree, mostly as flag garlands or large, flat, heart-shaped purses sewn together from two pieces of colored paper. The little purses were always empty, since anything placed inside would cause them to collapse.

The most unusual thing for me at Christmas were the ring dances, when Icelanders danced hand-in-hand around the Christmas tree. In their songs they maintained that they were encircling a juniper bush. It never crossed my mind to associate this misinformation with the mental condition of the asylum inhabitants. After all, they hadn't created the custom, and furthermore, it was found all over the country.

On Christmas Eve there was mutton and a large number of gifts—mostly children's books, and of course they were all in Icelandic. I immediately began to learn to read Icelandic, and to forget the German that only my mother and my brother could understand anyway. After about a half year, I had so completely forgotten German that just one word seemed to remain as a little remembrance. I don't know why, but it was the word for *Hosenträger* (suspenders). The meaning did not seem to play a role, since I had no idea what it meant. It was rather a matter of the length of the word. I got to know another boy, who, like me, had come from

Germany, and he too had unloaded the German language ballast. He had also kept one word as a souvenir, a word that was even more unusual than my *Hosenträger*, namely, the word *Pflaume* (plum). It is unusual because the *pf* is an uncommon sound in Icelandic, and is good only for expressing contempt. I wasn't impressed, and I said that my word was twice as long as *Pflaume* and thus I knew twice as much German as my opponent.

Learning Icelandic went so fast that I didn't even notice. Forgetting German went even faster and easier, and so communicating with patients and the employees in the hospital progressed with no difficulty. Both were familiar with unusual communication forms from everyday experience. I must add here that only later did I recognize the tendency of Icelanders to express themselves in a poetic and ornate way, revealing an unbridled joy in original formulations and resourceful turns of phrase. Words have for them more than a basic informational function, as we know it best in German imperatives. An Icelander weaves verbal artwork in the air; Germans, on the other hand, merely produce clear instructions. The former might seem to be for only useless personal reasons—sometimes even a brief misuse of the language, a twist and turn of phrase—while the latter serves a distinct purpose. The appearance is, however, often deceptive, for the joy of wordplay has helped the Icelanders though many difficult times.

When you come from Germany, you first have to learn to speak by wanting to say something. That's not all that difficult, since Germans are on occasion completely accustomed to wax poetic about deep but meaningless things. In Iceland it is also preferred to recite poems without any meaningful text, just so long as they rhyme or are somehow repetitive, and can be presented with singular emphasis. It sounds a lot like a broken record player. In that way you can take note of something that you actually don't have to know, or don't want to know.

The difference between the two languages followed me throughout my life and planted itself in my breast, and neither language wanted to make room for the other one. On the surface they are both closely related; sometimes it was just a matter of exchanging one or another letter, and suddenly an Icelandic word became a German word. On the other hand, from the inside, however you want to describe it, the worlds are completely different. This text is being written in German, and I am already having trouble with the words. Germans, to be sure, do battle with their words, while the Icelander merely plays with them. As a German I keep looking for an appropriate word; as an Icelander I look for a fitting meaning for the word. The Icelander is a words artist; the German is a builder. For the Icelander in me, rules are of no real importance, while the German is always looking for better rules.

This kind of thinking was still quite distant on my arrival in Iceland, and for the sake of simplicity, I think, I simply forgot my old German language and took on the new Icelandic. The fact that I essentially learned it from the patients in an asylum was no disadvantage, for, as I have already stated, at the core is artistic freedom.

In Iceland the intellectual climate for me was the insane asylum, and thus I saw this as Icelandic normality. I was well aware of the fact that most of the inhabitants were sick, but sickness is normal for everyone, even the healthy. Anyone who has never been sick, or who can't seem to get sick, isn't normal. To be precise, normally we are considered sick either when we are very sick (for example, cancer, instead of a cold), or sick in some unusual way— as are the mentally ill. In the first case, you get sympathy; in the latter case, displeasure. Displeasure excites the inhabitants of a nerve clinic or asylum, especially when they get on one another's nerves. They rile each other up and then, as is usually the case with people, they get louder and freer in their choice of words. Finally, when words are not enough, they begin to attack each other and become even freer in their choice of means for their attack. The art for the caretakers consists of recognizing as soon as possible the escalating interaction and thus to work against the developing chaos. First of all, it is important not to let yourself be taken in by what is happening, but to act in a soothing and understanding way. My mother seemed to have mastered this art in a very special way, and it may have been to her advantage that she could not get overly excited. It was impossible to get on her nerves, and that really got on my nerves. The power of loving people, one might have effusively called it, was what she was doing, but it was also her tyranny of goodwill. In any case, in an insane asylum in which everything—including today's pharmaceutics—revolved around quiet, my mother's ability to quieten others was a sensational gift.

She accepted everything calmly, even when her superiors suggested that her unusual gift be investigated scientifically. The only other way that inmates calmed down, it seemed to me, was their measured unrest in the form of swaying, rowing, or cradling themselves. Sometimes they just did this, but sometimes they clearly did it to calm themselves down.

Mother's half-restful women's area

Everywhere you would see patients swaying, rowing, and cradling, while some talked or sang softly to themselves. I thought a lot about that; I especially thought about the rocking chairs so beloved in Iceland and elsewhere, and that in the entire hospital there was not a single one—except for the chauffeur, Ásbjörn, who often sat in his and smoked his cigar. I wondered if his stoic calmness was a result of rocking. For the children, someone had put up a swing in the courtyard of the hospital, hanging it on the clothesline, and there I could try out the calming effect of swinging to my heart's content.

The dominant orderly element in the hospital was the two opposite poles: *calm* and *restless.* This was apparent even in the architectural design, and it helped separate the men from the women. As a result, there was a "very calm," a "calm," a "restless," and a "very restless" women's ward, and corresponding men's wards. Beyond these extreme ends of the calm-restless scale, the picture was quite different: at the restless end, there was something like a padded room where a patient could romp about without hurting himself or others and could not damage his surroundings. At the calm end, the patients were able to mingle in the normal society of the mentally healthy. This was carried out by design, since those about to be released were housed in their own somewhat removed building, *Viðihlíð* (Willowslope), a separate building at Kleppur. They could go in an out freely, which many did, while some simply took permanent leave of the asylum. Some, however, preferred the intimate society of those mentally ill to the outside community, itself nearly insane, and stayed.

Eva

One of those "very calm" and privileged patients, Eva Hjálmarsdóttir, a well-known writer, simply sat there in her bed and wrote her books until she died. My mother took special care of her, and so Eva wrote poems with an unusually comforting effect. I saw in her eyes something more lively, and this too she was able to put in her poems in an endearing and understanding way, and thus make her life bearable.

Eva was a fragile but absolutely inspired woman who was always well dressed as she sat in her bed near the window and pondered dreamily, looking somewhat sadly at the meadows outside. Eva was still a young and beautiful woman who was able to create wonderful worlds in her head, while I had to run around in the vicinity just to discover one world. But Eva could only talk about the wonderful worlds she created. For the most part, she put down a few shaky letters on her paper, and then had to wait for friends who would write down her words for her.

My mother explained to me that Eva had suffered in her childhood from horrible cramps and seizures that lasted several days. She was bound to her bed by a lameness that progressively got worse. The seizures were so strong and painful that she thought each time she would not survive. When I visited her, she beamed with cheerfulness and zest for life and seemed to have only one thing on her mind: to teach me correct rhymes. She told me that I created false rhymes, just as she had done in her youth.

Interest in rhyme schemes was not what motivated me; I wanted to know about the secret and wonderful world in her head from which she drew such strength and joy. It was so great that she wrote a book with the title: "*Það er gaman að lifa*"; translated, it means something like "It is wonderful to live." "*Gaman*" is difficult to translate; the meaning lies somewhere between *joy* and *fun*.

Eva said that she was happy every morning when she woke up early and knew that she had been granted one more day, even if it might cause her the most horrible agony. Sometimes I was overcome by the thought that she was the one who had freed herself and that I was the one who was bound, even though I could run around as much as I wanted to. I decided to look for these mysterious and hidden worlds, and to become a writer. I immediately began to write poetry and short stories, but I kept them under lock and key as my own secret. Only Eva, my teacher, was allowed to know about them.

Head Doctor Helgi

The society that took me in so completely, as a little runt, was unusual, to put it mildly, but I didn't notice this in any particular way. For one thing, I didn't really know any Icelanders beyond the walls of the asylum; for another, I had memories of the crazy house called Germany, although those memories grew pale and faded. The fact was also covered up because I had landed in an insane asylum, and because both sick and healthy people made up the social life of the institution.

The fluid transition from healthy to sick became blurred and disappeared before my eyes, in such a way that everyone was healthy, or sick, or really neither. Each one was just that way and the other one another way; one was consistent, and the other only sometimes.

This was also true for the personnel, including my namesake, Head Doctor Helgi, and for the inmates of all of the wards.

It was also very much the case for me too, without my actually knowing it. Just like my mother, I became a little wheel in the larger wheelhouse of the central Icelandic insane asylum. The asylum had been given the unusual-sounding name of *Kleppur*. For the German ear, this sounds a lot like *Klapsmühle* (loony bin). No real meaning, however, can be drawn etymologically from the word. *Kleppur* is perhaps related to the German word *Klippe*, and indicates a stony landscape. The *Klaps* in *Klapsmühle* is most likely related to the word *Hau*, and is used in Germany for someone who has a screw loose, who is really off his rocker. In Iceland, in any case, the word *klepptækur* (fit for bedlam) is a colloquial expression for people whose behavior is different from the common and the predictable. Nowadays it means someone who is "ready to go into the asylum." What is easy to overlook is the fact that this designation includes all of those who feel comfortable and at home in the insane asylum; all of those who feel well taken care of there and find others like themselves; all of those who are left in peace there by understanding their uniqueness and even learning to value it.

And so I quickly felt at home in the asylum; actually, from the very first hours there. It did not concern me that among the medical experts there was concern about the effect the atmosphere could have on my later intellectual and emotional development. They arrived at the honest conclusion that they didn't have an inkling of an idea about why they were so concerned. There might be good results from my living in an asylum, but there might also be questionable consequences, which should be avoided. I was a single case, since my brother was still too young to talk about mental problems, and so they simply decided to wait and see. The only solution was to spend time somewhere else, maybe with learning-impaired children. That meant in practical terms sending me to another institution, but that could be done only when I started to school.

Boys from the Asylum

For psychiatrists too it never just rains, it always pours. The administration was confronted with another and very similar case. One of the nurses had danced her way out, mutated into a married woman, and then returned as a single mother back into the bosom of the asylum. They discussed her son Hörður, who was my age, until they were exhausted and finally came to the same conclusion—they didn't know why they were so concerned—but I got a playmate.

My mother calmly took note of this. For her, all the academically trained medical experts were just dear members of the asylum society, just like everybody else. Her biggest worry was looking after my little three-year-old brother who had become enormously mobile. The grounds of the hospital were not exactly a kindergarten playground. The builders of the asylum had chosen the location presumably with the ulterior motive of making it difficult for the inmates to secretly slip away. On two sides there were steep rocks that crashed down into the ocean, on a third side there was brackish water blocking the path, and on the fourth side there was a cliff fenced off but with a gate. The gate always stood open and had rusted in place.

The solution that my mother decided on for looking after my brother was quite typical for her mysterious relationship to the mentally ill. Even the hospital administrators were speechless. She located a babysitter, but what a babysitter it was! His was named Árni, he was skin and bones and was more than two meters tall, about six feet six. He worked otherwise in the furnace room of the institution, shoveling coal, and so his face and clothes were mostly gray or black. For most mothers this would have been reason enough to doubt Árni's fitness to babysit, but it was his prehistory that took the biscuit: of all of the permanent residents of the asylum, he was the only murderer. To be sure, he was no ordinary murderer. His misdeed had probably awakened in one and then another Icelander those proud memories of old and heroic times, when young Vikings sailed off to foreign lands and fought their way to victory with their swords. Árni had been a farm laborer —nothing specific is actually known—but the farmer treated him badly and lorded over him, maybe even in an insulting and belittling way. In brief, on a beautiful summer day, while mowing hay with a sickle, Árni used the same implement to mow the farmer's head off. And so Árni then landed in Kleppur, probably because he did not show any remorse, and didn't do or say anything that might have explained his deed. This evil deed was commemorated by someone with a pile of stone, right in the middle of the field where normal deeds were never noticed, and where flowers sometimes marked good deeds.

It was this same man that my mother chose to look after my little brother. It was, one might say, a daring decision, for, aside from his dark past, Árni was not exactly able to develop a repertoire of skills dealing with people while shoveling coal for the furnace. He came across as intimidating if not threatening, especially if one knew about his past.

Only a few people had ever heard him utter a single word, and no one really knew if he could smile. Árni and my energetic little brother got along with each other splendidly, from the very first time they met. One day the horrible fears that many thought would someday happen, seemed about to come true. My mother casually looked out of the kitchen window of the semi-calm women's section where she was the director. She stopped what she was doing, as if struck by lightning, let out a carefully measured cry of horror, opened the door and locked it behind her, and ran down the steps out onto the asylum's courtyard. There stood Árni, tall and thin as he was, dark gray and black as always, and in his large black claws he clutched my brother. Árni had four of his black fingers in my brother's gurgling mouth—two at the top and two at the bottom of his teeth—pulled his mouth open as wide as he could, and was probing as deeply into his throat as he could. "*Helvítis titturinn át skrúfuna,*" he continued to say, beside himself with doubt. Translated that meant, "that damned weenie ate the screw." What he meant was the iron nut that Árni had given his protégé to play with. My little brother, as is usually the case, lost it, and Árni's great fear was that he could have swallowed it. Nothing would do but to give him a complete once-over! My mother, of course, quickly understood the situation and was able to calm Árni down. If my little brother really did swallow the rusted lump of iron, he handled it quite well, and there were no apparent aftereffects.

Such happenings as this one were quite unusual, and they would have caused us to doubt the ability of some of the inmates to behave rationally. Certainly some of them behaved in an unusual way, but that didn't make them forget who they were. Their behavior was unusual because nobody else behaved that way, especially no one outside the institution. They remained faithful to their rather slanted view of life, something that we might sometimes call character. We could count on them, just the way you can count on someone with a more acceptable character.

There was, however, one small problem: the problem of an inmate's changing character. The doctors spoke about seizures. Some patients had two characters, so to speak: one who was calm, while the other one was unruly.

During the calm phase there was no reason to lock up the person, but in the unruly phase this was advisable. The problem consisted in finding the right time for both of these actions, especially when the transition from the one phase to the other took place quite unexpectedly.

The most prominent case of this kind in the hospital was a man named Valdi. Valdi would have been called an original if there hadn't been so many competing originals. Even so, he stood out as most unusual among all those with unusual personalities.

Valdi

During his calm times, Valdi was a wanderer; actually, it was a little more than that. He was a free-rower, for he was the only patient who had a little rowing boat at his disposal, and he often rowed out into the sound to go fishing.

Valdi's boat

We young boys learned everything from Valdi that one can and should know as an Icelandic fisherman, including chewing tobacco—but it didn't taste good to us, and we didn't tolerate it very well. Icelandic fishermen, according to Valdi, do not smoke tobacco, nor do they dip snuff. The sea mist puts out the tobacco fire and the cigarettes just hang unattractively, wet and limp, from the corner of your mouth. Dipping snuff is also a frustrating matter on the high seas. Scarcely is the tin open when the tobacco is blown away by the ocean breeze, leaving only crumbs to put where one really wants it—namely, in the nose.

There was one other thing that we learned in detail from Valdi: the continuous swearing that was fitting for his social standing. In all likelihood about three fourths of what came out of Valdi's mouth every day were swearwords. But what an abundance there was!

Valdi's swearwords were artistic, far beyond any base grammar and any kind of banal poetic meaning or lofty poetic creations. He wasn't simply communicating something like some kind of genuine Icelandic poet; swearing for him had its own noble reason—art for art's sake, so to speak. He didn't just curse someone or something, not even the weather or just everything in general. Successful swearwords as long as your arm made him out to be the happy creator of a unique work of art.

As someone who was on the borderline with language anyway, I immediately noticed a difference with the Bavarian swearing that I knew from home. It was a difference as large as heaven and hell, in the truest sense of those words. A swearing Bavarian is caught up with heavenly happenings in both his thoughts and his words. *Kreuzhimmelherrgottsakrament* (Christ and God Almighty sacraments) is one of the most beloved Bavarian cuss words. On the other hand, the Icelandic swearer prefers to deal with the underworld: *andskotanshelvítisdjöfulsins* (damned bloody hell) was the way he preferred to begin his cussing. Valdi had expanded this basic expression, this universal swearword, and built it in a seemingly Dadaistic manner to some kind of artistic system. The words that he took up in his swearing repertoire all lost their original and base meaning and were poetically ennobled as swearwords. It seemed to me that all of his swearwords must have been created somewhere near a fireplace, for every word that was taken into his swearing-cosmos had something to do with heat and fire and thus with the kitchen. *Eldur, brennandi, sjóðandi,* and *logandi* (burning, boiling, flaming fire) were regularly repeated vocabulary. The German swearer could compete only with his meager *Teufelsbraten* (devil's roast).

In Valdi's swearing there were certainly interesting ingredients, varied kitchen utensils and kitchen activities such as slicing and sewing up, and skewering and flattening out. Sometimes I thought he might be able to turn the entire Icelandic language into one swearword, even write a swear-novel, which of course only he would be able to understand. (But maybe *understand* might mean something completely different, something cursed.)

For days I listened to Valdi and tried in this way to learn Icelandic, but then I found out that Valdi just swore to himself as the words came to him. It was always about something—maybe the ultimate and absolute swearword—that would change Valdi's world like a magical charm would, with one fell swoop. It would be something like the password for entry into a wistfully hoped-for beyond. As is well known, Icelanders of old hung on to their hopes for what awaited them in the beyond with considerable difficulty: every day they had to kill one another off, and in the evening drink their mead to get their strength back, just to be able to begin once again on the next day, happily, with their bloodbath.

I learned from Valdi to deal with grammar rather freely, since it seemed to play no particular role for him. His swearing was more like a hymn of praise, free of formal limits—a majestic ode, a gesture of grandeur being directed toward something, possibly something apocalyptic.

With time I was able to open up to Valdi's art of swearing, and I could then be happy about the new and meaningful ideas, as he was too. One moment of glory came for me when Valdi, on one occasion, right in the middle of a cannonade of swearwords, lost his thread of thought, and because I had listened to him so dutifully I was able to supply him with the missing phrase. He looked at me, full of disbelief, just as if he had suddenly met up with himself. Then a smile softly crossed his face and he said, "Thank you." I had the feeling that he was thanking me for much, much more than just the missing word.

In his wandering, Valdi was more than just a boundary wanderer. From time to time he suffered from an inner turmoil that was then acted out in an unusual wanderlust. So that he wouldn't get lost on land or sea, he was kept at home until he calmed down again. As one might imagine, this did not make him happy, and so they tried to put off the time when he would have to be locked up. In later years, Head Nurse Guðríður asked me secretly how it was going with Valdi, and whether his artistic swearing offered any signs that a period of unruliness might be anticipated. I had misgivings over and over again. I didn't want to squeal on him and have them lock him up prematurely, but I also didn't want to be responsible for them not removing him soon enough from the scene, enabling him to leave and then get lost. Using his swearing as an indication of his moods didn't prove to be very reliable. I could indeed see changes in his poetry of swearwords, but there seemed to be no real connection with his phases of wanderlust.

CHAPTER THREE

Exploring

It was necessary during the first winter after our arrival in Kleppur for me to explore the huge building. Staying outside in the open air in Iceland is not always advised for young children. Sometimes it storms to such a degree that you are forced to crawl around on all fours, because visibility is so limited that you can get lost between your house and the garage, or, as Icelanders call it, stay outside. Kleppur lies exposed on a little spit of windswept landscape, and the winds are so strong that the public transportation omnibuses, called *Strætisvagnar* (street wagons), can be blown off the road on their way there. The buses then lay on their side in the ditch, looking foolish, until the wind died down and other buses could pull them back onto the road. The mishap usually took place in a nearby meadow, on the way to the hospital, resulting in a problem since the bus always tipped over on the side where the doors were. For the passengers the only way out was through the windows, not everyone's cup of tea.

When the weather was really bad, the huge hospital with its many corridors became a playhouse for the children. The locked doors to the unruly wards were certainly an obstacle. Locked doors were of course only for the patients, not for the personnel, and children were not calculated into this equation at all, since they were neither patients nor personnel. It was clear that we wouldn't get keys, but nowhere was our entry forbidden. We just had to work it out with the patients and the personnel. I soon realized that the children were—at least I was—a part of the inmates' lives, and they had become a part of mine. I felt responsible for them, and they paid attention to me—or at least they took notice of me as part of their community.

Without being especially conscious of it, I assumed the attitude of my mother toward the inmates: I took on responsibility for them and their fundamental and worried well-being. It wasn't pity that bound me to the patients; it was much more something like a feeling of belonging together and of a common fate. These weren't patients that lived in a hospital, at least not in the sense that they were suffering. It was much more like a closed society, with special rules, customs, and some freedoms. The members of this community got sick and then got well again, just like those on the outside of the hospital, but this did not affect the reason why they belonged to the asylum society. Most of them seemed to me to be at peace with themselves; even the troubled depressives seemed to be either satisfied with their situation, or they simply had no opinion about it.

The relationship to the world of the healthy and normal in the city, or out in the country, could be described as very relaxed. Visitors, common in most hospitals, were virtually never seen in Kleppur. Visits to town for those inmates who could get around easily, were not an especially exciting topic. The door and the gates were open for them, but only one inmate wanted to make use of it. His name was Steindór, and he was the only patient who owned a bicycle. It was assumed that he pedaled to town every day because he liked to ride his bicycle, and there was nowhere else to go.

Riding a bicycle in Iceland means a steady battle with the wind and the weather, especially with the wind. When it is difficult to walk without leaning into the wind, it is nearly impossible to push a bicycle, not to mention riding and balancing oneself on it.

I sometimes asked myself what it was that connected Steindór to his rusty old bike. It wasn't love; otherwise, he wouldn't have left the monster for us to practice on. The frame was so large, and our legs so short, that we could reach the pedals only by positioning ourselves "under the bar." This meant that we had to assume a certain slanting position, and that for only a very short period of time. This also meant that we soon landed in the ditch or slammed into the wall of a building. Neither is good for a bicycle, and it came as no surprise that traces of our accidents were left on Steindór's means of transportation. That didn't seem to bother him at all; on the contrary, I got the impression that he was glad that his bicycle had finally acquired some meaning. He patiently and with great joy repaired the bike after each crash, and then took up his routine trips to town again.

Everyday life in the asylum was a strange mixture of rules and exceptions. Actually, the entire undertaking was an exception, but there were strict rules that made the exceptions into a stable order. But that was not enough; even the rules that steer the happenings in an insane asylum along regular paths were also subject to exceptions, which then could become rules, if they were desirable; to put it mildly, it was all rather crazy.

Carnival (Shrovetide) in Iceland, which follows the Christmas celebration after a proper time period, is a fitting example for the exception to the rule. As Lutherans, the Icelandic people have something of a split relationship with Catholic customs. As forced converts who were fundamentally against force, they came out of the confessional wars somewhat misshapen. Some thus seek spiritual refuge among the tried and tested gods of their ancient forebears; for others, it was just folklore; and still others take what appears to be useful to them, from wherever. Especially beautiful baroque-Catholic traditions are part of the confusion of customs for Easter; that is, around the time of Lent, even though this primarily reflects the taste of the Protestants. The most beautiful to be sure is the time of Lent, or just before it begins.

The fun-filled festivity celebrating solemn abstinence begins in Iceland on the Monday before Ash Wednesday; in German it is called Rose Monday. It begins in the ungodly early morning hours with a kind of castigation. Fully dressed people are supposed to beat completely naked people with specially prepared torture instruments, with brooms that remind everyone of the instruments used in the Catholic church to sprinkle holy water on the members of the congregation. But this rather crazy custom was never conducted according to its original form. Today, the custom consists of children making artistically shaped brooms from colored paper that they acquired at a specialty shop, setting the alarm clock at some un-Christian hour, and then pouncing on their sleeping parents and shouting wildly "Bolla Bolla Bolla," and beating them with the *bollundagsvöndur* (wands, on Monday: pancake day). For the parents, the only way to stop this is to purchase their freedom by making a loud thud-like noise themselves (*Bollern*). For every successful hit on their parents, they are given a chocolate-marmalade-cream-filled carnival fritter. These can be bought on *Boller*-day in every bakery in town. The children get their punishment in the form of various kinds of stomachaches.

On the next day in Bavaria, Fat Tuesday (Mardi Gras), the custom is more in line with Icelandic straightforwardness. Here one might be suspicious of Danish complicity in introducing a bombardment of calories. Tuesday is the day of manly meals and heroic eating according to the best Viking customs; that is, until the eaters burst open. And so the day takes on the appropriate name *Sprengidagur* (bursting day: Shrove Tuesday). Based on experience, the best foods are salty meat and beans as propulsion fuel.

On Ash Wednesday this horrific episode it supposed to be over, but that is not quite the case. Once again it is the children who set out to torment the grown-ups. They are now armed with little bags filled with ashes, and they then sneak up and hang them on the coattails of their unsuspecting parents. What is most unusual about this Icelandic custom is that nobody seems to know what it is supposed to mean, and so the custom is even crazier than the two already mentioned.

The survival of this unusual custom has become problematic because of an increasing lack of ashes, and apparently because of a better quality of pins. They have become ever sharper and are bent into little hooks for hanging them at the bottom of the pant's seat, and that has led to a kind of parental acupuncture.

It was easy for me to learn about such new customs, but my mother insisted that I leave the patients alone, especially those who were bedridden. I had to concentrate on the personnel, but here I met with craziness of another type, just more cooked-up and thus less productive. I was richly rewarded, however, by refocusing on what took place up in the hallway of the hospital attic. This "Hall" was in constant use during this festive time. In addition to the personnel, entry was permitted for all those who were not locked up, even some of the patients who came from the secure but calm wards.

By far the most desirable activity were the movie shows, and the best of these were the ones that were the craziest: silent movies with Buster Keaton, Charlie Chaplin, Abbot and Costello, et al. All the patients from all the wards were allowed to come to the movies, and so here the fun could hardly be controlled.

Even the more serious films caused the viewers to roll in laughter. You could count on it; someone always laughed. So, no matter what was happening on the screen, at least one person would find it comical. What troubled me most was that the projectionist, a pudgy little man named Viggó, seemed to be infected by the viewers' laughter, and himself laughed throughout the film. He really seemed to enjoy these presentations. Viggó's name clearly fit with *bíó*, the Icelandic word for movie theater. He was a friendly little man who had great difficulty dragging his equipment up to the attic of the hospital. His attitude revealed the fact that he was not particularly happy about this situation, but it was clear that his mood got better during the showing of the film.

The same kind of happy effect was obvious from the dance balls that took place up in the attic during these festive days. They were primarily for the personnel, but guests also came, especially the trusted patients. *Ball* doesn't necessarily mean the same thing in Iceland as it does elsewhere, especially in Germany. A more fitting word would probably be *dance-event,* or *party.* The planning of the dance was what was important, more or less. During this time, dances resulted in excitement and some scares. Icelanders, one might surmise, were more fit for doing battle, even if only with the forces of nature, than for dancing.

Out in the countryside, people preferred to go to so-called meetinghouses. Here all the dancers stayed around until midnight, by which time they had drunk enough to get into the swing of things. The women at the dance—those who did not participate in the drunken revelry—sat around patiently knitting. The drunkenness unfortunately didn't last very long, and thus the balls ended after one or two hours, when the police arrived. This was sometimes quite dramatic. Because there were not enough jails—there was only one in all of Iceland, and it was chronically filled up—the schnapps-laden bodies were put in big woolen sacks that were then hung up on large hooks in the slaughter house. Swaying back and forth in the hammocks, they could dream about the fun at the ball. The main problem in having a ball was the fact that alcohol was prohibited. The guests at the ball were thus compelled to spend much of their intellectual energy, which they could have used for cultured conversation, and devote it to alcohol smuggling. At the balls, coffee and lemonade were always served. In addition, there was something called *öl* (beer) or *maltöl* (malt beer), but this had about as much to do with beer as axle grease does. To Germans, this drink is more like the malt extract prescribed for mothers recovering from childbearing.

The balls up in the attic of the Kleppur hospital were quite unusual, without any noticeable accomplishments, no time limit, and without any hint of failure. They started around coffee time in the afternoon, but really were no different from a regular coffee klatch. The seating had been placed around the walls so that there was a dance floor in the middle, and in the corner a record player droned on. In the course of the ball, this record player took on increasingly less importance, since the guests liked to bring along their own musical instruments. But here they were just as creative as they had been elsewhere with smuggling alcohol. Some played a comb, or sang through the spout of a coffee pot. What they liked most, however, was banging sounds, drums, or any kind of percussion instrument: tin cans, tin dishes, wooden boxes, and such. Some sang, others whistled or hummed, and everybody danced. Some directed the music, others directed while dancing. To my ears it was a wonderful concert, and so I must assume that it was also pleasing to the ears of the musicians and the dancers. After every piece—they always stopped just when the record ended—everyone applauded enthusiastically.

Carnival at Kleppur

As strange as it may seem, this polyrhythmic noise chaos didn't seem to upset any of the patients who were there, even though some of them were known to me to be on the borderline between the different kinds of wards. On the contrary, those from the calm wards perked up, and those from the restless wards relaxed. The excited ones appeared dreamy and calm—at least, they closed their eyes and had blissful smiles on their lips. Others who usually stared absently into emptiness just stared at each other and grinned.

The ball ended just as unspectacularly as it had begun. The guests disappeared, one after the other, or began to clean up. The last dancers kept up the beat in time to the music, in a soulful trance and cradling each other.

I think it was at one of these nearly mystical gatherings that I began to think about where I had landed. My world was an insane asylum, and everything that happened there was just as natural as life with a family in their village was for other children. I knew that it was different out there, that people outside behaved otherwise, but "different" was there and "normal" was here. In my world, there were people who year-in and year-out simply repeated the same words, just as the head doctor did. People in my world threw themselves at a padded wall until they sank down to the floor in complete exhaustion. There were also people who never opened their mouths and thus got their food through a tube inserted into their nostrils. People lived there whose behavior never caused any surprises, and there were those who were capable of doing something unexpected, again and again. Outside it was boring, forceful, and regulated. Often it struck me that the inmates were freer people, but only sometimes. Perhaps, I thought again, the sick are just locked up in themselves, or maybe they aren't even locked up, they just don't want to leave their inner life behind. Many appeared to be very content with their fate, or at least they were not openly unhappy. Many were stopped from leaving the institution, or at least their ward, but they were left alone in their inner world. No one tried to penetrate it or mold them to do differently. They were left in peace, as long as they didn't harm others.

One cannot really say that the asylum inmates were indifferent to each other. Their community was more like troops than a family or a village community. Their society was always provisional; they formed a community thrown together by fate, and they did not think about the meaning or the purpose of being together. They didn't even think about the fact that they were shut out, locked in, and separated. There was a dominant conviction that being closed in was for their own good. They were patients in need of care and protection, even from themselves.

The dances in the attic had awakened my curiosity: was there something up there they were hiding from me? Was I the outsider who was being kept out so that I didn't bother them? Did they have secrets, a secret inner world, maybe even a common one from which I was being excluded? Somehow, I thought, I had to gain entry to this hidden world; I must understand even those who babbled meaninglessly to themselves. My control figure would be Rúna. Rúna seemed in every way quite normal. She was a normal kitchen assistant, industrious, friendly, content, and obedient. She helped my mother in the dining room by dishing out the food sent up by elevator from the central kitchen down below. It was prepared in portions for the patients in this ward and dished onto the appropriate plates for eating. It was here also where the thin and tasteless brew was prepared before it was funneled to the motionless patients through the nose.

Rúna was something like my mother's right hand, and, because I liked to hang around the kitchen, she soon became my favorite conversational partner. There was, however, a certain story behind this, since Rúna was only externally a conversation partner. Inside Rúna was another conversation partner who talked with her, and sometimes with me. It all depended on whether they had the time and were not conversing with each other. I set out on my goal-oriented research of Rúna's inner life by giving the two internal Rúnas different names. I called them "Rúna *þessi*" and "Rúna *hin*." This meant simply *this* Rúna and *that* Rúna. I first tried it with Rúna *one* and Rúna *two*, but that broke down when the two Rúnas were not ready to accept these names. I also had difficulty with *this* and *that*, as can be seen in the following recreated dialogue:

H: Good morning, Rúna, how are you today?
R: Great.
H: And how is <u>that</u> Rúna?
R: Which one?
H: Well, the other one, the one you always talk to.
R: Who do you mean?
H: Well, not <u>this</u> one, not you, but <u>that</u> one.
R: That's me, dear Helgi; you seem to be a little confused today.

It was like the old story between the hare and the hedgehog, and as the rabbit, I didn't have a chance. It also didn't help to try to talk to both at the same time, as the following dialogue shows:

H: Good morning to both Rúnas; how are you today?
R: Good morning, Helgi; are you talking to me?
H: No, I am talking to both of you.
R: Is there somebody else here?

I had to think about another tactic; maybe it would be better to take her by surprise and confront her.

H: Rúna, you were just talking to someone, I heard it. Who was that?
R: It was me; I was talking to myself.
H: But I heard that you were arguing with someone.
R: That happens; I change my mind sometimes.
H: But so very fast!
R: How else?
H: Well, maybe slowly, gradually.
R: I don't like halfway opinions.

I didn't get very far this way, either. The two Rúnas continued to talk with each other, get into arguments, and even scold each other fiercely. One day I found out that they were talking about me and how I could have come up with the crazy idea that there might actually be two Rúnas. Finally I realized that I was on the wrong path. It wasn't just two people, like Valdi and Árni, who were talking inside Rúna's head; it was much more a case of Rúna *þessi* and Rúna *hin*, but both of them were in fact Rúna. Rúna *þessi* knew everything that Rúna *hin* knew, but they were nevertheless opposites.

I was in the process of learning an important lesson; namely, that anybody who claims to know what he has to learn is getting in his own way. It is especially important to keep your eyes open when you fail. Happy is he who takes it this far and doesn't fail.

I stopped my attempts to understand the insane and started showing them more respect. I ceased trying to associate their thinking with my thinking and to explain it, and began to get involved, with growing amazement. Sometimes this opened up worlds to me that were both strange and familiar. Simply, I did not ask, but took part, thought along with them, and didn't ponder further. Nothing much came from this, and so it didn't really work, but I enjoyed the variety and the discoveries, and I learned to value and seek out my own special world.

The craziest world in the entire hospital was up in the attic of an attached second building, the *Gamli* Kleppur (Old Bedlam). This doesn't mean the decrepit part; rather, it means the old part of the hospital. This older building had been constructed in a traditional way, mostly from wood and corrugated iron, and had a gigantic space under the roof truss; but it hadn't been turned into cell-like rooms for the employees as it had in the other building. It was spacious enough for a row of bunks to be put in up there. In order to let some light into the darkness, large windows had been built in, and more light came in from various hatches. The row of bunks took on the architectural character of low row houses. These beds were occupied by bearded old men, seamen, who were accustomed to such accommodations, and thus were happy up there. For unknown reasons, they became stranded in an insane asylum without really belonging there. They led their own lives, got their meals from the institution's kitchen, and let time pass there, much as it does on the open sea.

Sometimes they told stories, repeating them at irregular intervals. Sometimes they were just friendly, but they were always fascinating because of their long beards and their mysterious appearance in the half darkness of the little area up in the attic, with storms raging outside.

Sometimes I just sat in this cramped space and listened to them telling stories. When one of them talked, it seemed like he was talking for everybody there, but the others didn't appear to be listening, just following the sound and the rhythm of his voice, like listening to the sound and rhythm of the waves along the coast. They already knew all the stories and maybe even the most varied ways of telling them. They just liked the ritual, like the rolling of a boat on the ocean. Once again I was reminded that language wasn't being used here to communicate something to the others. They were all speaking softly, except for the one telling the story. They were united in their speaking the way people are unified through singing.

It sometimes happened that the monotone singsong put me to sleep. The stories themselves were not especially exciting, the soft glow of the light bulb dimly lighting the room—all this simply made me sleepy. At some point, one of them would wake me up in a friendly way and let me know that it was time to return to the world down below. There were times when it seemed that I was about to return from this normal world into a crazy world, to descend from this calm and reasonable setting, as reliable as the pendulum on a clock, down into a world off its rocker, where the unforeseeable was common, and surprises were the rule of everyday life. To be sure, it was an exciting world down there, but it was also a very lively one. The attic, on the other hand, was calm, distant, and sleepy—perhaps maybe a little too much, perhaps monotonous, too harmonic, too slow. Missing was the lively dissonance of the underworld, the thrill of the unknown, the sheer joy of skirting the rules. Already on the way down I started to miss the musty and spicy smell of wood in the attic; I missed the feeling of traveling through time on an ancient ship with ancient Vikings. I found myself back in the confusion of regular life and began to look with new curiosity into the nearest corner.

The deeper one descended in the hospital, the earthier life became. In the cellar you could find everything that kept the entire institution going. Through my own musing I could find some kind of order, an orderliness which was manifest organically, and through the smells down there. In the cellar it was possible to walk from one end to the other of the entire hospital and see its workings. There were random and crazy corners that probably had something to do with the construction of the building or the architectural design, but it was still possible to move about unhindered. I was able to pass through the institution's kitchen and go past huge, burning-hot frying pans, bubbling and steaming giant cook pots, and clattering potato-peeling machines, not to mention the kitchen personnel who bustled around with oversized ladles and cooking spoons.

At the upper, the noble, end of the cellar, was the asylum's brain center, and at the far end of the brain sat the head doctor. He had my name, Helgi—which surprised me just a little—because the brain's family name was *Rannsókn* and translates simply as "investigation." It was here that the medical personnel, mostly students and the two senior nurses, spent their time. All power emanated from them, especially from Guðríður, the senior head nurse, the undisputed queen of the asylum. The translation of her name is something like "God on a horse" or "God rides." In her case, it couldn't have been better chosen.

Head Nurse Guðríður

Guðríður was born to be a ruling figure—beautiful and sovereign, equipped with the irresistible aura of a person who believes with every thread of her being that she was doing the right thing, the good thing; rightful goodness, so to speak. Guðríður, this head nurse, was my mother's best friend and our neighbor. And so, in a special way, I was subject to the compelling power of what was right and good, a condition one can deal with over time only if one also looks at the other side. Guðríður's underlings were very good at looking briefly at her instructions and directives and getting around them with fantasy. She didn't like that I quickly adapted this behavior and learned to follow her wishes without placing my own too far in the background.

Like most nurses, the ruling head nurse was always thinking about health, and especially about the health of those patients who were assigned to her. From this and other things, a kind of tossed salad of conflicts developed over the years. In the first place there was oil, and then there was vinegar. This senior nurse shared the opinion of most of the local people, that salad was a kind of grass and thus it was animal fodder. The most important trait of salad, in her eyes, was the green—or in the case of tomatoes red—color used to enhance the color of meat, fish, or potato dishes. Since it was used as decoration, oil and vinegar was unnecessary and even detracted from the taste. This salad-conflict was solved diplomatically by putting the vinegar and oil under the salad and served to the senior head nurse from above.

Halldóra, the lesser senior nurse, was primarily there for logistics, and managed, among other things, the asylum's lemonade depot. That made her something of a key figure for the children, far more important than the white queen, as we called the head nurse.

The doctors, notoriously bored, sat in the observation rooms around a large table, told jokes, and drew pictures on notepads.

What else were they supposed to do! The inmates lived from day to day under the careful watch of the nurses, and were for the most part quite healthy. The reason they were in the asylum never played a role in gauging their health, particularly not in the sense that they might get better. My namesake, Helgi, a self-declared friend of humanity, vehemently rejected more meaningful measures such as were practiced everywhere abroad. And so in Iceland, no one ever tried to help depressives by driving a spoon-shaped piece of iron through the eye socket and into the brain, where it was twisted around. The head doctor could also not convince himself that electroshock therapy could be used for healing, and thus the patients were spared having someone try to fry their brains.

The only healing method to be employed, if anything at all was used, was time and the self-healing powers of human nature. Otherwise, the doctors and nurses tried only to make life in the asylum at least worth living, for the duration, and for all participants.

Thus examinations were not really necessary, and so the doctors sat in their examination rooms, much like in a waiting room, doing nothing, and were happy when there was some kind of interruption in the daily routine. My mother was able to utilize the services of the head doctor, to look into my notorious headaches. She was worried about them, but I had long since come to terms with my fate.

My own explanation was that my skull was simply too small for my brain, but nobody wanted to accept that, especially not the head doctor. I was sent to his private examination room, that otherwise served as a junk room. There I had to allow him to knock around on my head, and it is understandable that he found nothing, but my mother seemed to be satisfied. I asked myself later what she might have feared, but we never discussed the examination.

The dangers of the lower floors, where the doctors reigned, I had not at all forgotten. Once, when I caught a terrible cold, I was chosen as a defenseless guinea pig for a new American wonder drug by the name of penicillin. Every day at the same time, one of the students, called "candidates," appeared at my bedside—in his white robes—and gave me a huge shot of this new active agent, presumably enough for several Icelandic horses. Finally I got well, anyway, but the medicine had proven itself in the eyes of the candidates.

Somewhere in the middle kingdom of the cellar, the kitchen elf Laura reined. Her official title was *ráðskona* (housekeeper), which one might actually interpret as ruler since the political ministers in Iceland were called *ráðherrar* (minister). In any case, her department contributed much to making life in the hospital worth living. She could magically put each and every unusual Icelandic culinary specialty in reliable quality on the table: first in the little canteen next door, down in the cellar, but then throughout the entire house, all the way up to the quiet little sections of the attic.

Coming from Bavaria and war rations, I had difficulty in the beginning with these unusual foods, even though they satisfied the heart and the stomach of every Icelander.

Most troublesome was the fish, and other creatures of the sea, like whale flesh. I really had stomach trouble with the rotting ray fish that was served up on Friday, in honor of Catholic fasting restrictions. In Iceland, Friday is still referred to as fasting day. You don't even have to eat the dreadful thing to get sick; a light odor coming from that direction is enough to make the stomach turn.

Other dishes merely needed getting used to, some more, some less. Among the more difficult ones to get used to was candied blood sausage, no doubt an inheritance from Danish culinary art. Icelanders liked to preserve their fat-laced blood sausage in sour milk; if it wasn't eaten up immediately when it was first prepared, it was then served along with liver sausage. I actually knew this pairing from Bavaria.

Eating parrot-perch and some kinds of turbot that looked like swimming bulldogs only brought on mild fears of an unsettled stomach, as did an unusual and ancient wart-covered fish called a *Grausleppa* (gray female lumpsucker), probably because its flesh is gray and has the consistency of slimy jelly. It is a delicacy for Icelanders, but it took some time for me to get around to seeing it that way.

The Icelandic cuisine has a certain refinement, but it is easy to think that the defining taste nuances are all associated with successful preserving methods. They especially love the old way, salting it down. Drying in the prevailing wet climate of Iceland was never a very successful undertaking. Soaking it in sour milk, when this was available, was certainly a more sure way to preserve food.

Wood was needed for smoking, or sheep manure, but the latter was also needed for making a fire. A gourmet preferred the manure taste in the smoked meat.

Icelanders prefer the head of the sheep as a specialty dish, and prepared it the old Germanic way. Once again you can detect their tendency toward cultivated barbarianisms; in order to get rid of the hair on the face of the sheep, it is not shaved away but is held over the fire so that the hair burns and produces the typical smell of burning hair. The sheep's head changes color, much as burned bodies do, and becomes jet black. Only when singed in this way is the sheep's head a favorite food for Icelanders. I was able to participate only in a limited way, and so I left some parts (the eyes and the tongue) for people who had higher intellectual abilities, such as my mother.

Singeing of sheep's head

Laura, the queen of the kitchen, had mastered the entire—the most distinctive and traditional—array of Icelandic specialty tastes, but in no way should she be considered backward. Still, this didn't go so far that she would serve new kinds of food, like lobster or mussels. Tradition-bound Icelanders shuddered at the thought of these, just as they dreaded chicken. Chickens, I thought at one time, were for laying eggs, not eating. You don't eat dogs or cats; horses, yes, at least those that were not named. Lobster was used only for bait to catch cod, and mussels were to be eaten only just before starving, if at all.

The worst of all of the food that came from Laura's kitchen was, in my opinion, the *Hræringur* (porridge with yogurt). Just the name brings to mind unappetizing associations; its appearance was worse. It looked suspiciously like the slime that was fed down through the nose of coma patients. *Hræringur* sounds as much like *hræ* as it does *hrákur*, one means "vulture" and the other, "spittle." It doesn't help much that it actually means "scrambled," like the mixture made of oatmeal and *skyr*, Icelandic yogurt. I find it impossible to say what it tastes like without making the reader ill. I don't think Laura was responsible for the *Hræringur*, for sure, she didn't create it, even though it did come from her kitchen—but many of the misguided liked it so much that she even sweetened it.

The little mortuary

Beyond the kitchen came the actual inner workings of the hospital. Here there were processes important for our livelihood: receiving food, storing it, and getting rid of garbage. Even the heating furnace was down there, wall to wall with the cooling room. Just outside the back entrance-exit there were two buildings; one was the mortuary, the other was the pig sty, right next to piles of coal, a woodpile, and a continually smoldering ash heap.

The mortuary fascinated the children, as did the pig pen, but in different ways. The one building cast a spell over us; it was open but couldn't be entered because of the smell. The other one was closed, and we never knew if it was occupied. One was filled with squealing life, and the other just the opposite.

Actually everything, except living people, came in through this funny back entrance-exit door to the hospital, or left from there. It landed on the garbage or the *Öskuhaugur* (ash heap, refuse dump), in the mortuary, or in Ásbjörn's black panel wagon. This rather imposing vehicle was something like a life-sustaining umbilical cord between the hospital and the city. Otherwise only a tired old horse pulling the milk wagon came to the hospital every morning, or sometimes a farmer who took away the leftovers from the kitchen. Ásbjörn's truck was the only possibility for the children to leave the hospital, at least on their own.

Ásbjörn and his panel truck

We didn't have a chance as stowaways because Ásbjörn was always looking out for such attempts on our part, but he was a good-natured man, and we knew how to exploit this side of his character. We paid dearly for one such adventurous trip out into the world, since we had to find a place to hide somewhere in the back of his old crate. At that time, this was not an uncommon way for people to travel. Everywhere one could see trucks with little homemade huts built into their beds. These huts resembled an omnibus, and people were transported in them much like on a bus. The structures were for some unexplainable reason called the "body," and were like a wooden and homemade, more or less successful Jeep-carrosserie, part of the street scene at that time in Iceland.

The stay in Ásbjörn's truck was anything but a pleasure. It was easiest to take when stopped completely, so that Ásbjörn could pick up dirty laundry and take it to a central washhouse near Landsspítali and bring it back when it was clean. It smelled horrible, but, without these soft bags of laundry in the truck, we would have been thrown around on the bumpy dirt road to and from the city, to the point that later we would not have been able to sit down because of the pain. With some self-discipline we got used to the smell, but not to the bouncing. The smelly part of these adventures was not limited to the dirty laundry or the penetrating soap smell of the clean clothes, but also included the food stuffs that Ásbjörn had to transport every day, especially the fish that he picked up in the fish market at the harbor. Included with all this was the indispensable cod liver oil, which really rounded out the bouquet.

In spite of all these smelly impositions, I enjoyed the trips with Ásbjörn because I could get some idea of the city Reykjavik and surmise what all might be found there, as soon as I could go there on my own. But for the time being, I was like all of the other inmates at Kleppur, limited in my ability to move around on the institution's grounds.

CHAPTER FOUR

The Real Crazy House

I spent the summer every year with my grandparents on their farm Heiðarsel in Skaftafellssýla. When I returned to Kleppur in the fall, my mother told me something quite shocking: they had decided that I would not only go to the elementary school (called *barnaskóli* in Iceland; i.e., children's school) in Laugarnes, but that I would also live there in a home. Protesting was useless. It was, so to speak, a Supreme Court decision, arrived at by the all-knowing decision makers of the insane asylum. They had all agreed that it was to my benefit. According to everything known by psychiatry, psychology, and pedagogy, there was no precedent, and anyone who grew up among all kinds of crazy people would certainly learn all kinds of crazy behavior and would thus become crazy himself. I would have countered that the crazies, here where I was growing up, had not grown up among other crazies—for the most part—but rather among healthy people, the non-crazies; but my opinion didn't count.

Many years later, my mother told me that they all recognized that I felt very good in the community of those mentally ill, actually at home there, and they had even noticed a certain healing effect of my presence on many of those who were ill; but they had also viewed this connection to the disturbed as a kind of danger for my own intellectual health. In a word, and not so good for me, I was sent to a home associated with the Laugarnes Elementary School. It was about three or four kilometers from the hospital to the school, but for me there were vast universes between them.

In Iceland, students normally lived at the school when the distance to get there was too far or too difficult. This was quite common for those who lived in rural areas, but it was seldom the case for children in the city. The reasons for sending me to this boarding school were of course quite unusual: I was living in an insane asylum. Today we would talk about problematic families, or about children who were difficult to educate being sent to boarding school, but that was not why I was sent across town to be educated. Here, school-age boys lived in the same building where their classes were. The youngest were seven years old, like me, while the oldest were from twelve to fourteen, depending on how often they had been held back from promotion.

The shock following my delivery to the school was, one might say, of a political nature. In stark contrast to the insane asylum, there were very strict and sometimes brutal hierarchies here. Supervisory personnel were present, but here it was not a mild and loving benevolent caretaking that the individual was subjected to, but rather a pitiless and police-state strictness that prevailed. This actually seemed to be necessary, since the subjects of this small police state were anything but docile and obedient. Valdi would have called them devils, all of them.

It was difficult to adjust. It soon became clear to me that in this community, there were higher-up and lower-down individuals; there was a very rigid pecking order, and there were firm rules about how one moved up and down within the system. Everything revolved around this hierarchy.

The most important means for social climbing was the ritualized struggle for rank, fighting. If at all possible, these fights would be arranged for and acted out in public. In this way it was possible to choose between freestyle—that usually meant common fighting—and special, more respectable types of battle, but these were also subject to certain modes of fighting. At about the time of my entrance into the boarding school, a special kind of wrestling was popular. It consisted of the two adversaries putting their arms around each other and then pushing the knuckle of the opponent's twisted thumb into his backbone. If it were done anatomically and skillfully, the adversary would fall down with a horrible cry of pain. This particular method of determining rank was relatively effective, and the result was clear, since it was seldom the case that both fighters screamed in pain and fell down at the same time. In the freestyle, it was different: stalemates were considerably more frequent here, and wounding was frequent. Establishing rank could be worked out only after long discussions, if at all.

Freestyle, however, was also subject to many rules. It was, for example, forbidden to use weapons of any kind, like stones, sticks, food, or muck. Pinching, tickling, spitting, pulling hair, to name just a few things, were also not allowed. Sticking to the rules, and thus verifying the validity of the battle, was carried out by onlookers.

It occurred to me right away that the strongest boy could be challenged, even though that was not a very good idea. But you also didn't have to begin with the weakest and thus fight your way up, step by step, in the hierarchy. Rather, it was good to look for a couple of equally strong opponents in order to test your own ability and thereby gain some idea where you might fit into the pecking order. It was natural that a new student would set an avalanche of fights in motion, unless, of course, he was a weakling and always occupied the lower end of the scale. There was never any period of calm, since everyone was always trying to better his rank.

In addition to these hierarchy battles, there were a few others, with relatively little effect, and less-violent means for social climbing. There were, for example, associations with the more powerful protectors, something like a league of mercenaries. In this case, property could play a major role. Real or merely ascribed abilities could also bring about a change in one's rank in the hierarchy. This was particularly the case for those at the top of a rank order, the ones you had to approach with respect and submission. Among those of lesser status, stories circulated, mostly about their very limited criminal acts, but also about their special abilities like making the future come out the way they wanted it to. For this they used the knotholes in the numerous new buildings that were being constructed around the school at that time.

This is how that went: Icelanders live their lives always expecting earthquakes, and so they build their houses so that in every situation they don't have to fear how much will fall down on their heads. This is no small matter, since the lighter a roof or an upper story is, the more easily a storm will blow it away. The earlier residents lived in earth houses with sod roofs, and nothing was blown away, but a lot fell down on them. More recently corrugated tin was the preferred way to build. It was light and blew away quite readily. The newest solution to this dilemma was concrete, made for the centuries, but it had to be poured into wooden forms. That meant that a double-walled house was built out of sturdy wooden boards, concrete was poured into the opening between the two walls, and then the wooden structure was torn down.

In these narrow wooden constructions there were naturally a large number of knotholes, and these had a magical meaning for my fellow school comrades, comparable to the Wailing Wall in Jerusalem for Orthodox Jews. It was a matter of finding an appropriate and, if possible, unusual branch, using it to take the core of the branch out of the knothole, speaking one's wish into the hole and then placing the core—marked as occupied—back into the knothole.

The procedure was no guarantee that the wish would be granted; you also had to have the right connection to the powers of fate. Such abilities were attributed to the leadership team, and they talked and acted as if they were the high priests of this community of belief.

I found myself confronted with a strictly vertical social order and had to try not to stand out.

It was, I soon learned, not a good idea at all to draw the attention of the warlords to myself. If I could just take up my position down at the bottom of the hierarchy, so I thought, then they would leave me in peace. That was a mistake, as I soon discovered. I was continually attacked by the weakest, the handicapped and the suppressed, all of whom hoped to escape from their whipping boy position, bringing up the rear. And so I was compelled to prove to them that I wasn't hesitating to participate in the free-for-all out of weakness.

I could have guessed it: I was undermining the system in a major way, but I was lucky that the powers-that-be still hadn't taken note of me. That would come soon enough.

In the beginning, the fights were not my main problem; rather, it was the unusual daily routine, including nights. During the night-time hours, the boarding-school groups divided into upper, middle, and lower strata with an especially brutal clarity. The interior architectural design of the sleeping rooms contributed in a nearly fatal way to this situation. To save space, it had been decided to put in three tiered beds, and because they were conceived of for children, they were not very stabile. This made an enormous potential for social conflict.

Following the basic laws of society, whereby everything good comes from above, the "upper boys," the nobility of the home society, took the upper-level beds, and down below was where the underlings slept, or didn't.

Precisely this arrangement brought on acts of violence of the worst kind. The poor devils in the lower bunks had great difficulty sleeping. Many wet the beds, and so it was advisable for this reason to quarter them close to the floor and not over the heads of their roommates. Others talked loud nonsense in their sleep, moaned, wept, or suddenly let out a shout. Still others—and this was reason for drastic penalties—began in their sleep to rhythmically rock back and forth. This rocking motion, following the laws of physics—and bad carpentry—was felt up to the topmost bunks, and then the poor construction was even more obvious. Neighboring beds were also in motion, whether by physical or psychic resonance, and so the nobility in the upper beds were rolled back and forth and were always in danger of crashing down from on high.

What happened in the semidarkness of the night lighting was nothing less than a beating of the weakest ones. It ended when the weakest of the weak, a retarded boy with a bald and much-too-small head, had to take a drink out of his own chamber pot. Secretly I thought, at least it was his own.

The days were easier to deal with than the nights. This had primarily to do with the fact that the mornings were taken up by schooling. I began to love school, even though I still had some problems with the language. The only thing that really caused me trouble was the inescapable cod-liver oil, the smell of which I knew already from Ásbjörn's stinking truck.

Icelanders believe in the powers of cod-liver oil the way Bavarians believe in the powers of pork roast. In order to assure that the daily dose of this stinking elixir is officially controlled, the task is not left to the sometimes-slipshod mothers to pour it into a child's mouth; it is the duty of the school.

This disgusting ritual was carried out daily in the following way: the school nurse brought to the first hour of class, from whatever source, a white enamel one-liter pitcher filled to the brim with cod-liver oil. To set the mood, it was placed on the central heating register so that a delightful aroma could develop and then penetrate the entire room. When it had reached the right point, and the teacher could begin filling up his students: he took out a yellow cloth from his desk that helped him forcefully hold down the chin of the boy about to be filled up, just as Árni has once done so violently with my little brother. The procedure often caused difficulty for the teacher. Sometimes a child would get the fish-oil in his nostril, or some other place, and then spew a liver-oil fountain out like a geyser, all over the cursing teacher and his school comrades.

It is difficult to say which was worse from this Nordic fountain of health: its smell or its taste. Worse than both, in any case, was the aftertaste. This was so pungent that even the home directorship, usually committed to the Spartan, showed some understanding: in order to get rid of this horrible aftertaste, we schoolchildren were given a little piece of rye bread, with about three centimeters of crust, to chew on.

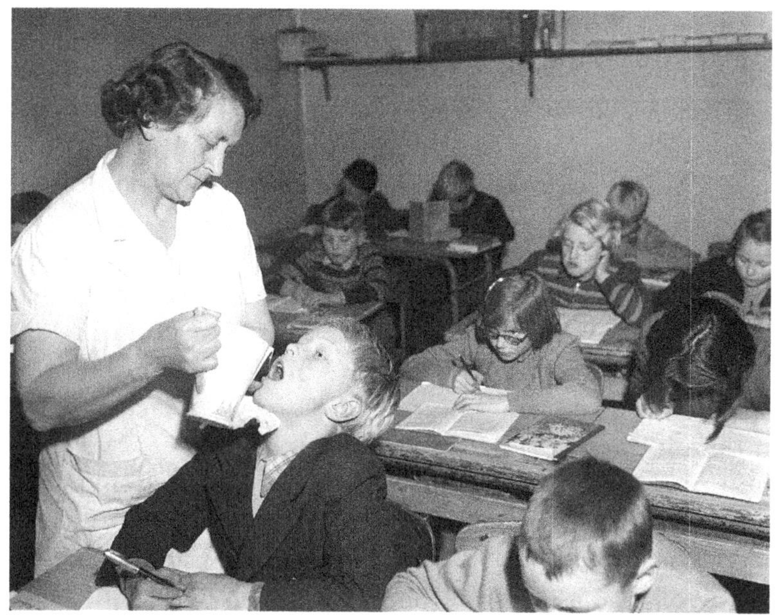

Nurse pouring in the elixir

We were not supposed to be taught like weaklings, I thought; we were to be educated according to old Viking ideals. Maybe we were indeed chosen to join an army of fearless warriors for something good or the like: courageous, hardened, boiled clean. Apropos boiling: every week with horrible regularity a boiling action took place. We were stripped down naked and led one by one into a bathing chamber. Waiting there, sitting at the edge of a steaming bathtub with a sarcastic smile on their faces, were the Valkyries who worked in the school. There was no getting away; the room was very small, and the Valkyries wore special rubber gloves, the surface of which was covered with suckers like those on a squid or an octopus. With these she locked on to her victims and dunked them into the soapy brew in spite of all their screaming, pleading, and stomping. Hel, I remembered was the goddess of the underworld, and it could not have been much worse down there. The children entered the torture chamber pale and wan, the way Icelandic children are, and came out as red as a boiled lobster. No wonder Icelanders don't like lobsters!

The bath torture was not the only hygienic high point of the week in the boarding school. The second was engineered by the school director herself, presumably because of its far-reaching mythological effect. The director was fittingly named Vigdís, which meant in translation something like battle maiden, or simply Valkyrie.

It had to do with cutting fingernails. In no country in the world does this procedure have such a doomsday meaning as in Iceland. In order to understand, we need to look deeply into the traditional Nordic belief system. The old Norsemen knew about a hidden but divine wharf where a mighty ship was placed on its keel, and in time it was to hold all of humanity.

The uniqueness of this ship was that it was patched together from the finger- and toenails of dead people. As soon as it is finished, so goes the unshakeable belief of the ancient ancestors, the world will come to an end. Modern Icelanders question such prophecies because everyone knows that it can happen in a different way from what one thinks. And perhaps in such a way, they think that the ancients maybe weren't always wrong.

So, because the senior Valkyrie of the Laugarnes boarding school thought her role was to educate potential warriors for doomsday, I didn't take any chances and cut my fingernails as short as possible, thereby delaying the world's downfall as much as I could. She, however, carried out the procedure behind closed and, for the most part, soundproof doors. The children were led in to see her individually and returned this time not completely red over their whole bodies, but crying and with bloody fingers.

All of this, and a lot more, took place with the best of intentions and concern for our health and well-being. It was never pleasant, and I couldn't find any pleasure even in the obligatory light treatment. In this case it smelled like ozone, and it was terribly boring. Once again we had to strip down naked, which was actually quite pleasant, because I got to take off the itchy wool underwear, always stinking like sheep's fat, for a short period.

What then happened, to put it mildly, was stressful. For a long time, you had to lie on your stomach, then for a similar time on your back, and so on. We weren't allowed to talk, just to listen to a nurse who had come especially to see us. She read something she thought was really funny; at least, she laughed the whole time. The children didn't understand anything—at least, I didn't—but to be truthful, I could see that it was even more boring for the poor nurse than it was for us children.

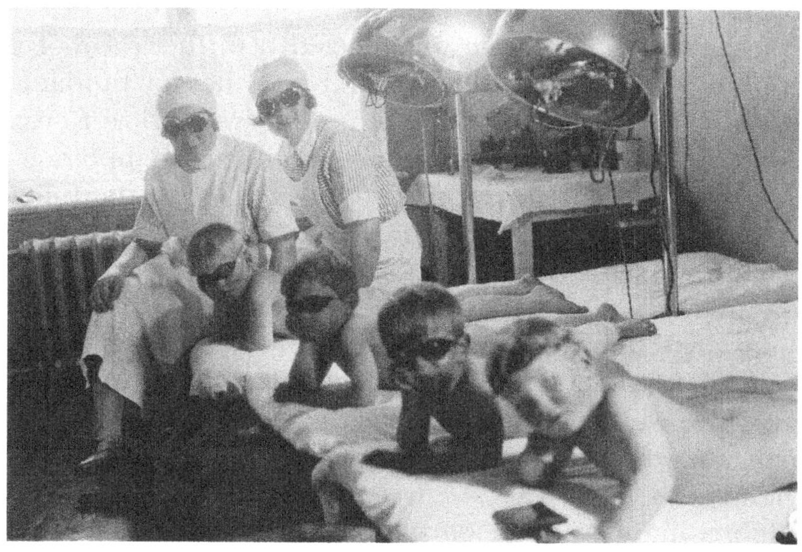

Light treatment

During my time at the boarding school, my social position gradually became more aggravated. I came into the line of fire by the upper echelon, and for more than one reason. They noticed that my Icelandic revealed certain peculiarities that could be explained only by my unusual background, whether from Germany or from the insane asylum. My obvious tendency toward peacefulness, and especially my indifference to the hierarchy, did not fit into their worldview at all. For me, the warlords were just one of the many variations of the ever-present normal craziness, whether that madness was inside or outside the asylum.

In any case, I provoked them by trying not to provoke them. I did not cross their paths, somewhat like avoiding a mad dog. I didn't stand in awe of them, didn't hate them, and was not afraid of them. I gradually dropped out of the system, which bothered them even more. Then the ultimate evil came about. Those lower down began to see in me something of a pioneer, as one of them who would stick his tongue out to the oppressors. I was wandering around in a minefield; the social tension increased from day to day, and it seemed that the bad guys were just waiting for an opportune time to teach me a lesson.

The confrontation came unexpectedly, in the guise of open proof of my supersensory abilities, and with that my fundamental otherness. This wasn't good for me as an insignificant creature in a lower-school class. The completely unusual happening that could not be explained with reason, took place in the following way: school had just finished, and I was strolling along as I did every day toward the dining hall of the boarding school. For some reason unknown to me, I was in a better mood than usual and was swinging my school bag—more accurately stated, I was spinning it around my arm. With Icelandic schoolbags that was possible, because they were carefully made for growing children and were as small as a woman's purse. The schoolbooks are also small, thin, and light.

While swinging the schoolbag like a propeller around my wrist, I walked into the dining hall, and that was when fate set out on its own path: the handgrip slid off my wrist and the satchel went flying up to the ceiling. There it hit one of the many tubular lighting pipes that were used to illuminate the hall. The pipe separated from its base, even though it shouldn't have, and fell to the floor. With everyone looking on, the unbelievable happened: nothing. The tube bounced around a couple of times, from one end to the other, and then just lay there, undamaged, on the floor. Virtually every mouth in the hall remained open, whether empty or full. Well, and what was I supposed to do? Say I was sorry? I did what seemed to be the most advisable; I acted like the entire episode didn't concern me, as if it was just routine for me, that the tube had not been properly attached, and I had gotten rid of it.

Later it was difficult to say whether I had more good than bad luck in the matter of the falling pipe. It was bad luck that the satchel got away from me, that it hit the pipe, bad luck that the pipe was not put up very securely, but it was good luck that it didn't break, and it was very good luck that it hadn't already fallen on the head of a student or into his food. What happened, however, would have to be counted as bad luck, or at least a fateful necessity. First came the joyous applause of the lower and middle strata, but then the increasing and growing rancor of the upper stratum. Finally the gullible young ones thought of me as a magician, and thus for the ruling class it became clear: the time was ripe for my public humiliation. I had to be shown my place; I was to be made aware of the official order of things.

That was abundantly clear to me, and in the beginning I did not try to change the course of what was happening. I spent much more time thinking about how to steer the unavoidable and highly embarrassing humiliation onto a course that was bearable. Outwardly, the upperclassmen were of the same opinion and thus thought about how they could get this unappealing situation behind them without escalating it, and, if at all possible, not bringing the school and other adult authorities into the matter. They invited me to a discussion, or better said, they summoned me to their court. They were not unfriendly at all, and actually treated me with a certain respect. They behaved as if they were acting unwillingly, but trustingly carrying out a higher mission. It wasn't something that concerned them personally; it was, rather, about something higher up, something more encompassing.

It was through them that society, the system, was articulated, and I could not extract myself from this authority. There was no small corner that I could personally retreat to, where I could withdraw and watch the action as an unparticipating observer. I could understand the boys, in a strange way; they almost made me feel sorry for the way they had to look for a humiliating punishment to keep me in check.

When they had seen my basic willingness for their action, they were visibly relieved and put their heads together to consult.

It didn't take long before they had a course of action they had decided on, and then they revealed it to me in a ceremonial but still questioning way. My dreadful punishment was to consist of milking a free-range mare out in the pasture. I was amazed and somewhat relieved at the same time. I knew how to deal with horses, those that were more or less wild, from my grandparents' farm. I agreed to their judgment, and the court breathed a sigh of relief.

The punishment was carried out the very next day. The matter had been spread around among the school population, and so, as expected, the gapers stood around, full of expectations, out by the designated horse pasture. I was led into the arena by two strong fellows, one on my right side and the other on my left, and once inside the fence I was left to my unsure fate. A few horses were grazing peacefully; among them, a reddish-brown mare with a colt. She was my goal and my fate.

I pulled up a bunch of grass from the meadow and approached the unwitting animal with a friendly outreached hand, letting out with some kind of comforting sounds. Getting close took place with no difficulty; the friendly animal sniffed at my hand and allowed me to run my fingers through its mane and stroke its back.

When I thought I was near enough to its rear end, I bent down abruptly, took a teat, and pulled on it with force so that it could be seen from far away. The mare seemed to need a moment to grasp this idiotic turn of events, but then she acted like she had received an electric shock. Up front I could hear an unusual snorting, and out back the rear rose up as if punching holes in the air. I drew back as quickly as I could, and the horse galloped off in the opposite direction, followed by its offspring.

I did not have the feeling that I had accomplished some heroic act, but this was clearly the opinion of those schoolboys gathered around. Their applauding and shouting could not be missed. The system henchmen were somewhat impressed, but didn't seem to grasp the amazement that their younger classmates showed me. The affair, at least I thought, still wasn't completely finished.

My decision was firm, however: I would leave this insane asylum and go back to Kleppur to my friends. The decision was as easy to make as saying good-bye. A few days later, I set out on my way home, away from the boarding school. I knew which way to go, and I took the most direct route over a stony but confusing hilltop called Laugarholt. No one seemed to have noticed my disappearance between the new buildings near the school. The path seemed to be longer than I had expected it to be, but probably because I kept turning around to look back to see if someone was following me. Far and wide, no one was to be seen. After about a good hour, I could see my goal, Kleppur. In the distance, white in the light of evening, the insane asylum looked to me like the legendary castle of a prince in a fairy tale.

At the doorway I was greeted by Árni, who was visibly touched to see me. I explained the situation to him briefly and asked him to frighten off any possible pursuers from the hospital grounds by scaring them mildly. Personally I just wanted to wait out the developments, and so I withdrew to the older people up in the loft of old Kleppur.

What then happened I know only from hearsay. It took a little while before my disappearance was noticed at the school. In spite of all of my careful measures, one of the little ones had observed my departure and then spilled the beans when they began to ask about and look for me. Vigdís, the battle maiden, was beside herself and made the mistake of sending two of the oldest warriors out to find me. They were, first of all, not very bright. After several tries, they had not been able to finish up at the elementary school, and secondly, they really didn't think that I would seek refuge by going back to the insane asylum.

But it happened as it had to: the two dumb warrior hit men who knew that I came from Kleppur, marched right over, crept around the building, and were discovered right away by Árni. He didn't have to do much to put the fear of death into my two pursuers. They tore off and fled for their lives, not back to where they came from but in the opposite direction, into the rocky landscape from which Kleppur once took its name. They hid there until dusk came and Árni went away.

In the meantime, Vigdís had recognized her first mistake and already made the next one. She sent two of her Valkyries out after the two dummies. The Valkyries were for the most part afraid of the insane asylum and its inhabitants, and when they arrived, Árni was still running about in his best frightening mood. They didn't get the job done, either, and returned on the next bus to the boarding school. Now Vigdís did what she should have done in the beginning: she called Kleppur and got Guðríður, the head nurse and my mother's closest friend, on the line. She told my mother about what had happened and she knew immediately where to look for me. I didn't care: I was happy; I was back home with my friends.

My mother was friendly but caring, as she always was, and had me examined right away. I was awaited by Guðríður and Helgi the head doctor, their faces not at all so menacing as I had imagined up in the loft.

Unusual behavior seldom caused them to lose their calm, and they couldn't really see much difference between my case and other cases there in the hospital. In their eyes I was rather something of a daily occurrence with less difficulty. They listened to my story patiently, attentively, and, as I saw it, with understanding. When I expressed my opinion that the boarding school in Laugarnes was the real crazy house, not Kleppur, Helgi smiled broadly, and I had the feeling that he believed me.

For me, what was important was that I didn't have to go back to the school. There was a short telephone call to Vigdís. Apparently she was happy to be rid of the center of unrest there. The two scared henchmen showed up before nightfall, and order was then returned to the boarding school.

From this point on, I had to take the *strætó*, the official omnibus, to school—more trouble than pleasure. In Kleppur I got the feeling that everyone was pleased about my return, and had actually missed me.

My mother really needed me to look after my little brother, since his Viking temperament was flourishing splendidly in the fresh ocean air. In his case an uncompromising joy of adventure and bodily fitness were joined in a frightening and almost legendary way. In addition he had an uncontrollable need for freedom and rejection of authority of any kind. The radius of his activity could scarcely be limited by rules or cautions of danger, and so it became my task to keep an eye on his doings, or, better said, to participate for safety's sake. During my absence at the boarding school, he had located a few very interesting and equally dangerous playgrounds. Following his Viking inclination to the sea, all of these places were at water's edge or in the water. For the most part it was ships, or at least parts of ships, that were of interest to him. Among them there were some very impressive ships that lay in the bay of Kleppur; all had been grounded from storms or some other enemy action. Near the shore was the front half of a giant Liberty ship; the back half had been lost somewhere in the Atlantic.

Ship graveyard

Icelandic trawlers had towed the remaining front section into the nearby ship graveyard called Keilir. To get on board we had to cross a hundred-meter-long hanging bridge that blew around wildly in the wind. It was difficult to cross it when it was iced up, even when there was no wind.

On shore there were several dozen wrecked warplanes that actually fascinated me more than the ships did. While I was busy trying in vain to tear out a souvenir with my bare hands, my brother had scurried across the hanging bridge and disappeared into the scrambled bowels of the warship. There were workers busy here and there on the site, but playing children were not part of their work assignment, and so they ignored us as long as we stayed on land. When we were on the warship, they were too lazy to follow us and were satisfied with a few volleys of cursing.

Onboard the wreck, we were met with a different world: rusted walls as high as a house, and black pits all around us. It reeked excitingly and in a familiar way of diesel oil, tar, rust, and seawater. We clambered over scrap iron and through pitch-black halls of iron, past canyons of metal and across swaying and moaning and creaking iron stairways, stinking and smeared with oil. We did this to our heart's content and as long as possible because we knew the price we would have to pay when we got home in the evening.

Iron playground

Apparently there was always a large host of protective angels looking over us since we were never hurt and not once did one of the welders working on the ship catch us. We could always figure out where they were, but they couldn't hear us much at all, and so it was no problem to keep away from them.

In addition to cannibalizing the ships, there was another playground on the other side of Kleppur that was equally interesting, called Vatnagarðar. There were ships there too, but more importantly there was a seaplane that on occasion was put in the water and then took off from Kleppsvík, the bay of Kleppur.

There was a broad concrete ramp for the seaplane and thus for us children a good place to go fishing.

For the most part, we could catch flounder and other flat fish, which we then took home to our mother as something of an unwelcomed gift. She should have been happy, though; we really didn't want to eat the fish.

It was always advisable for me to keep an eye on my brother, or to have informants keep him under surveillance, because his two favorite playgrounds were at least two kilometers apart, and there was no road connecting them. When the weather was bad—and that happens a lot in this little corner of the world—my brother's trail was easily lost in this broad expanse. However, in bad weather he could usually be found in the workshop of the carpenter Torfi, or with the housemaster and know-it-all Steini. Torfi, however, was not as impressed by this unpredictable little apprentice as was Steini. Actually, Torfi worked with modern machines, drills, crosscut saws and planes, with which one can work on fingers just as easily as on wood. With Steini it was far less mechanical, and he always had a vacant spot on his workbench where we boys could work on something. And we did this a lot.

Steini

Steini was very inventive, and he was especially gifted with small things. He was obsessed with making the objects of everyday life, especially tools that he produced in the smallest detail. He didn't really want to make toys, but rather teaching devices. The children of his day were supposed to learn to deal with everyday life situations by learning about the instruments of their ancestors. I already knew about this from the farm of my grandparents and much of this my grandfather had already rejected as modern stuff, even calling it the work of the devil. But I didn't say anything, because I didn't want to ruin my relationship to Steini. In Steini's eyes, I was a learning child, and in his opinion children were supposed to learn before they were allowed a point of view. In regard to their own opinions, that was a completely different matter, and so I quietly arrived at my own opinions. I fell into line with his ideas on teaching and built fascinating wooden miniatures from cast-off objects of daily use if possible: trawlers, for example, submarines and airplanes.

Model trawler

Steini would certainly have preferred pitchforks or sheep pens, but he resignedly let me proceed in hopes that I would one day find my way back to the old and trusted ways.

In spite of all this enthusiastic cultivating of tradition, Steini was an inventive, open-minded, and forward-looking man of the day. By retirement age he had developed a naturalistic way to produce artistic images. He began spreading out sand and gluing it to the canvas as his art surface.

Beautiful images of Icelandic landscapes arose, and the animals living there. Because they were waterproof they were very appropriate as decoration for bathing rooms where oil paintings were seldom found.

Steini was even successful making artistic creations out of the most modern materials, like acrylic glass, and all this in a most impressive and very popular way.

Acrylic plexiglas was something of a milestone in the history of the asylum; that at least was the goal when the sectional windows were embellished with it. It was probably thought that they would not break, that breakouts would thus be avoided, and that the ugly prison bars had always reminded the inmates that they were locked up. This proved to be only partly the case, because an unseen barrier was a hindrance to those patients who occasionally suffered from wild outbursts of rage and needed the reassurance and calming effect that comes from smashing glass. The effect of this invisible but insurmountable barrier worked only partially as planned. The fact that it was unbreakable brought some of those unstable patients into a complete rage, and they smashed, bent, and, in their heated state, threw everything there, from chamber pots to iron beds, at this unseen resistance. In the process the acrylic glass was not broken, but many fingers and joints were.

One of the last pre-acrylic glass breakouts in the history of the asylum was by a patient who really shouldn't have broken out. He was known all over the city as very dangerous. The occurrence took place shortly after my reintegration into the everyday life of the asylum. This unusually aggressive and unpredictable criminal had apparently seen it as his last chance to gain freedom and carry out a couple of despicable deeds before the acrylic barrier robbed him of his last hope. During one night he quickly smashed the unsecured window, including the transom, and disappeared into the dark.

Several of the nurses on the night shift flitted around for a while in the darkness outside the hospital, tripped, stepped in puddles, cursed, and finally woke up the head doctor. He called the police, but their night patrol decided it was too dark for a search. In any case they decided to keep quiet and not to warn the other inmates about this monster. First of all, this would have cast a negative light on the hospital, and second, it would have driven the inhabitants of the city crazy. All hope was put in the imminent arrival of daylight and the obvious white clothing of the escapee.

I participated in the excitement because my mother was on the night shift, and so I thought what I would do if I were the one who escaped. The matter of the clothing seemed to me to be a real problem, especially if they looked for me with an airplane, something that seemed reasonable in the treeless landscape of Iceland. To hide in an area covered with snow didn't seem advisable because of the temperature and wetness. He only had to systematically dirty up his clothing, something I knew a lot about. A few days later, when I gave my tip to the increasingly nervous doctors, I got only angry looks. Oh well, then they would have to get by without my help. But my curiosity had been awakened, so on the second day of the unsuccessful search, when the general population had been warned by radio, I felt called upon to participate in the search.

Journalists calculated repeatedly how far this brute could have gotten on foot by this time, who was in the danger zone, and most importantly recommended that the children should be kept at home. Doors and windows were to be closed and locked, and everyone was to prepare for the worst. I kept trying to put myself in the place of the escapee and let the search run through my head. While some thought that the escapee had perhaps stolen a car and driven over the mountains, I thought he could just as easily have stolen clothes, money, and a wig and be sitting innocently in a restaurant having a good time.

None of this seemed very likely to me. Perhaps, I thought, he hadn't really run away at all but was waiting somewhere in the vicinity with stolen provisions, food, and drink, until the search quieted down. The question was thus, where could someone hide in the area around the hospital? All of the outbuildings, sheds, and hidden corners had already been searched through many times, even the new building that was being constructed directly next to the main building. It was still filled with the lumber and other junk already mentioned, and it too had been carefully inspected.

Even so, I was drawn to it. The wind whistled around, cold as ice through the windows with no glass. It was wet and smelled like cement. The floor was covered with boards, all of which had nails protruding out of them that someone supposedly someday would extract. I was thinking again about something, or was looking somewhere other than the floor, and so it was with Johnny-Head-in-the-Air I was unlucky. Just when I cast my blank stare up at the ceiling, that's when it happened: I stepped on one of those cursed nails which then bored its way through my worthless rubber shoes and then through my foot. Precisely this moment of bad luck proved to be one of good luck: I spotted an inconspicuous little opening in the ceiling. It was not easy to see, but it had obviously been put in just in case someone really needed to get up into the flat loft.

I pulled the nail from my foot and the shoe and tried to suppress the pain with my quest for discovery. A ladder was quickly found and I hobbled my way up, step by step, toward the loft. The hatch was not locked, and I easily pushed it open with my head. It was pitch black up there, the only light coming from down below and up through the hatch opening. I had to pull myself up, hand over hand, in order to be able to see, then I had to wait for my eyes to adjust to the darkness. I crouched at the opening with my foot hurting me, surrounded by a thick forest of wooden studs supporting the roof beam. In the process I had forgotten to think about the problem patient and even why I had climbed up into this dirty lair. My researcher's urge, the foolishness of the discoverer, the ambition to have been there and to know that there was nothing there to discover, that and that alone stopped me from climbing right back down the ladder. It would have been a big mistake, for something rustled near me, and I could sense heavy breathing. No more information was necessary; I had found what I was looking for. Filled with fear and joy, I forgot for a while the pain in my foot.

Slowly my eyes penetrated the darkness, and the view that presented itself was such that the blood in the veins of a young boy like myself would freeze. I had expected a human being, someone who had made his hiding place into something comfortable. The sight that rose up out of the almost completely darkened space was that of a formless rising green monster. From this spongy mass two thin arms stuck out, and just there where I thought the head might be, I could pick out two eyes and a mouth. The bloodshot eyes stared at me, and an unclear and hoarse mumbling could be heard coming out of the mouth. It took a little while for me to gather my thoughts, and I briefly thought about just letting myself fall back down through the open hatch. All kinds of craziness shot through my mind: maybe it really was a monster, maybe it was the one being sought who was now so hungry that he would even devour children.... Then I experienced a sense of triumph: I had found the runaway, but now it was a matter of surviving the discovery and being able to tell about it.

I thought about my mother, and what she would do in my situation. I tried to convince myself that the thing before me was really a human being, just like you and me, even though it looked like a fairy-tale monster and was cold, hungry, and thirsty, and maybe even a little confused. I don't really remember any more just what I said, but it was surely something meaningless, like "They should have planned some windows up here," or "I stepped on a nail down below." It doesn't really matter what I said; the answer was more of that hoarse grumbling sound. Perhaps, I thought, maybe not at all wrong, that people dying of thirst always sound like that. That seemed to be the solution. "Wait," I said, "I'll go down and get us something to drink." Once again the same mumbling, but this time I thought I could hear a grateful consent.

Back down below I hobbled as fast as I could, blood flowing out of my rubber shoes, and down into the lower examination rooms. There it was busier than I had ever seen it before; strangers and police in uniform were there. I wanted to get as much as possible for my discovery, so I asked all around: "What'll I get if I tell you where the escapee is hiding?" I got only angry and even some worse looks, and they were just about to throw me out when someone spotted my bloody shoe and the trail of blood that I had left behind me. Doctors always react to such symptoms in a kind of special or compelling way. The sight of a bleeding wound forces them to turn to the one affected, especially when it is a child.

Easter was right around the corner and some jokester in the crowd shouted out: "If you tell us where he is, you'll get the biggest Easter egg that can be bought in the city."

That's was the right word, I thought! I revealed the hiding place, but not without mentioning that the runaway did not look like a human being but rather a green monster from a children's fairytale, and was suffering from horrible thirst. My business deal almost broke down because of this unnecessary additional comment, but the blood pouring out of my shoe lent my words the necessary credibility, and no one knew anywhere else to look, so they just followed the bloody trail.

I would liked to have been at the arrest, but because of my foot I was taken under treatment by the doctors, and in the meantime it was really hurting like hell.

Later they told me what had happened to the unusual, monstrous, and dehydrated image: it was green fiberglass that was being used to insulate the loft and was lying around all over the place. It was the only way the escapee could protect himself from the cold, and so he had wrapped himself in it, from head to foot.

I actually got the chocolate Easter egg, but I couldn't tell if it was really the largest in the city. It was, however, gigantic and wonderful, covered over and over with flowers and chickens made of icing.

Steini, the genial housemaster-artist in the asylum cellar, had in the meantime succeeded in utilizing those transparent and unbreakable acrylic glass panes for artistic purposes, even if they actually sometimes did break. He turned them into games of solitaire, by dividing them into manageable squares, then drilled little pits into the upper surface that would hold glass marbles. The goal of this solitaire game—called that because a single player has to contend only with his own understanding of the game—was to remove the marbles by jumping and thus capturing them until only one single marble was left.

This happens if one is lucky, and after several hundred trials, but then the player has bad luck because he can't remember how he did it. The game is really very good for entertaining oneself and for killing time. It doesn't really take a lot of understanding, but it doesn't really sharpen it either. It is thus, if you will, without any damaging effect, or it is "treatment neutral."

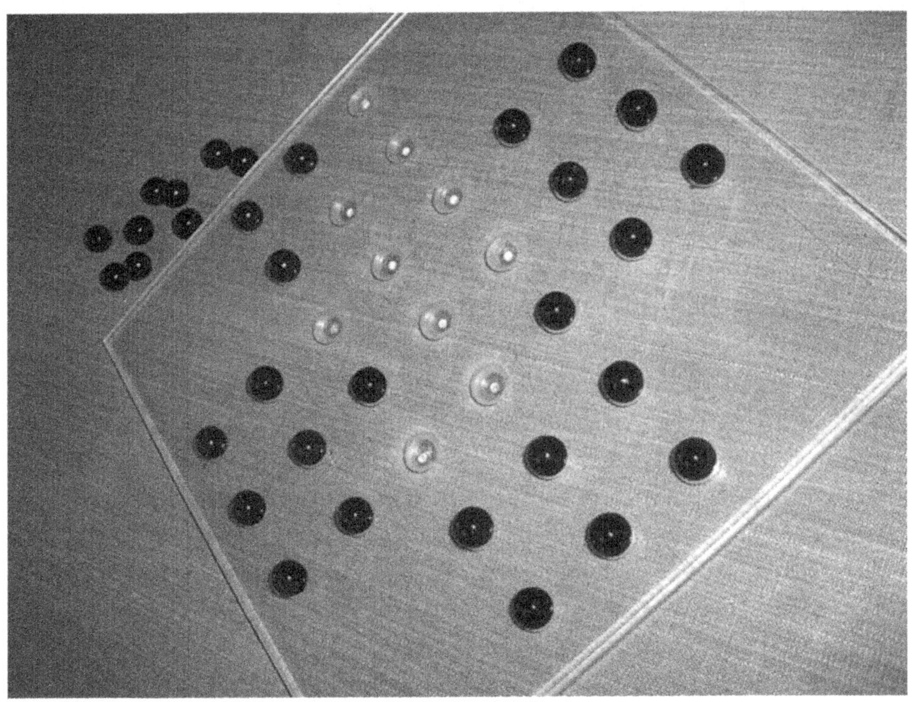

Acrylic solitary board

The game was very popular in the insane asylum, but it was good that the material was hard to break, since some of the inmates did not have the patience for mindless self-entertainment. Breaking the little glass balls proved to be even more difficult than smashing away at the acrylic boards. Some, however, expressed their idea that one or the other of the stomach acids would go to work on the unruly marbles if one simply swallowed them. The game became even more popular then because it could only be played under supervision.

Swallowing the game marbles as a rule did not cause the one who had swallowed them any trouble, but this was not so much the case for those watching them. My mother assigned me to this duty, to watch only those people who were suspected of carrying out such mischief. I learned a lot of interesting things about the relationship of patients to humor and digestion.

An older woman that I was to play the game with, and watch over, was under suspicion by my mother of swallowing the little spheres. I asked myself why she did this, and when she actually did it before my very eyes, faster than I could stop her, I asked her why she did it. First she looked at me surprised and acted like she didn't know what I was talking about. She grinned triumphantly the whole time and tried to make me out to be a liar. I knew that she knew that I knew that she had downed the marbles, but I also realized that she didn't really know why she had done it. Maybe she had just then realized what she had done when I accused her of it, but then was pleased with what she had done.

The matter—better said, the thought—became progressively more complicated. I looked into her eyes but there was no explanation there. I couldn't really believe my eyes; she had the marbles in her hand, brought them up to her mouth, and then they were gone. I maintained that they had wandered through the mouth and the throat into her stomach, but she said that they simply disappeared, which was actually true.

Well, OK, I thought to myself, I'll try again with another method, less easy to conceal, and see how she would react. I took one of the marbles and laid it on the palm of my hand while my game partner looked on carefully and a little astonished. Then I placed the marble in my mouth, as if to do just what she had done. At first my partner grinned, but then it appeared that another thought came into her head. A look of horror spread over her face; maybe she was thinking that the child had seduced her into swallowing the play marbles, but maybe she was really worried about the marbles, and about my digestion. With one swift move she stood up, knocked most of the marbles out of their holes on the board, and ran screaming loudly into the washroom where my mother was in the middle of dealing with the daily mountain of laundry. She directed her attention to the patient and not to me. She was finally able to calm her down, asking me to help her by telling her what had happened. I told her the truth: that I hadn't swallowed a marble, but the patient didn't want to accept my explanation. It was, however, a fact that one marble was missing. This suggested to my mother that the marble was indeed in one of our two stomachs; the only question was, in which one?

Later I realized that my mother apparently placed no more trust in my words than she did those of the inmates of the insane asylum. She actually believed that I would swallow a marble for no good reason, and then would lie about it even though there were trusted witnesses. No one but me seemed to be really interested in the truth, since that would have to be documented with considerable effort and cost.

Through such happenings I learned a new kind of truth, something like a private truth, and that I had to respect—at least according to my mother. To be sure—and sometimes this made the matter more difficult—one should see that this respect is based on mutual feelings. The best teachers in the matter lived up in the loft of Kleppur, but there I also experienced the limits of this new truth principle.

It was on one of these days, in the middle of spring, when one longed for the dry and sharp frost of winter. Down from the heavens came what Icelanders call *kaldi skítur* (cold filth), and this filth didn't just come down from heaven but also from below and from the side. This weather phenomenon is probably the main reason that Icelanders find umbrellas more scary than useful. On such days I withdrew into the inner reaches of the asylum, preferably to the loft above the hospital section.

The bearded old men around the table dozed in the dim light. One of them continually murmured something to himself, but nobody was listening. Time passed slowly toward the evening meal. I was reading an old newspaper, and wasn't really interested in the date, it appeared, but it was already quite yellowed and had obviously been used at some time to mop up spilled coffee.

The mélange of smells up in the loft varied from one time to the next and from day to day, but was always recognizable as the special air of the loft. On this particular day, I smelled it as never before; usually I smelled it when entering the loft space, but today I became aware of it right in the middle of the room.

I thought, it smells strange here; one could even say it actually stinks, not exactly to high heaven, but still.... This final limit seemed to be too quickly arrived at, for it began to stink something terrible. At first I didn't want to say anything about it because it might have offended my companions. Then I thought, they are sleeping, and so they don't notice it. "Fellows, don't you realize how it smells up here, ahh, stinks?" They looked at me through tired and sleepy eyes and one of them said, "And so?" Now I knew what this penetrating smell was; it was the singeing of sheep's heads. Who is roasting sheep's heads in this lousy weather? I thought, but the old men didn't believe anyone was doing that, and left it there. The odor got more and more pungent, not to mention unbearable. We are going to suffocate, I kept thinking. So, I said out loud, "I'll go see." Out in the hallway it was worse than in the room. Here the stench visibly hung in the air and could even be seen, like gray-brown clouds that wrapped around the beams.

The clouds swirled threateningly from down at the one end of the loft. This may be an insane asylum. I thought, but somebody's singeing sheep's heads in the dark; that is going too far. I did know, however, that back there was a large supply of horsehair. The horsehair was stuffed into the mattresses that the patients slept on during the night, and in some cases during the day. It was customary, for various and primarily hygienic reasons, to change it from time to time, to refresh it. The storage place was up in the loft, but here it didn't smell of freshness—quite the contrary.

I went around back and tried to let my eyes adjust to the haze and the darkness. What I saw took my breath away, more than it already had. Right in the middle of a gigantic pile of horsehair was a man, dressed in inmate's clothing, who was enjoying smoking a cigar of the type that I knew came from Ásbjörn: the panel truck driver. He casually shook the glowing ashes off into the horse-hair where they glowed happily, and were about to slowly start an extensive blaze. Smoke rose up from below, on his right and left. The man spotted me and was not impressed by such a little runt. Instead he made a couple of obvious gestures regarding what he planned to do with me if I didn't get out of there right away. I decided it would be better if I retreated and went to get help. In the meantime, it seemed that it had gotten too stuffy for my companions, and they came at me in the hallway as threatening as a herd of buffalo coming out of the fog, just as I had seen them in Roy Rogers's movies.

"We have to get help right away," I shouted to them, "there is a crazy man back there who is about to set the house on fire. Just think what that would mean! They would have to free all of the inmates in the hospital, the uncontrollable and the madmen! We'll have to warn them, and, to be on the safe side, we'll have let them all go outside so that nobody loses his life in the flames."

"Take it easy, not so fast," murmured the old men, "just don't overdo it. If the house burns down, then we will be the ones who did it. We will be the first ones affected; we will be accused of the fire." They had scarcely spoken when they all disappeared down below. I never thought that they could move so fast, but when there is the will even in old age they could move surprisingly fast. They had hardly gone away when they reappeared with buckets full of water. They didn't dither for long; they doused the stick glowing in the face of the smoker and then quickly climbed over the flames into the depths of the pile of horsehair. As soon as one emptied his bucket he ran back downstairs to fill it up again.

The delinquent was now dripping wet but was unimpressed and simply watched what was happening as he fumbled around picking up the pieces of his cigar. Apparently he was thinking how he could dry it out and save it. He could have spared himself such dreams, however, for one of the old men quickly took the *corpus delicti* out of his hands, threw it down, and trampled on it until it could no longer be seen in the other dirt on the floor.

When the fire had finally been put out, the next problem could already be seen. The floor of the loft was anything but waterproof, and most of the water used to put out the fire found itself on a path determined by gravity. It was obvious that soon there would have to be an inspection of the loft floor. The water would otherwise drip down onto the beds below and sooner or later it would be obvious to the personnel that its origin was not natural.

It had to have some kind of natural beginning, one that not even the cleverest nurse could associate with a nearly disastrous fire. Such an origin might be a hole in the roof and a driving rain. The rain, thank God, was already there, and only the hole in the roof was missing. The old men only had to loosen up just one of the sheets of the metal roof, and work on it a little. That seemed to please them. In any case they appeared to be very happy that their beloved domicile had not succumbed to the flames and they wouldn't have to submit to a brigade of investigators.

The dangers of smoking were made very clear to me, and many years later the smell of tobacco always brought back a lively memory of the stench of burning sheep's heads.

CHAPTER FIVE

On the Way to the City

The only means of public transportation in Reykjavik was called the *Strætó*, its full name being *Strætisvagnar Reyjavíkur* (Reykjavik Municipal Bus Service). These were buses, and one of them went every hour out to Kleppur, which meant that according to schedule, it traveled to the very end of the transportation network. When the weather was bad—and in Iceland that means a storm—and when the bus driver spotted such a storm, he turned around for safety reasons and returned to the city. In this way he avoided being blown into a ditch. For those passengers waiting in Kleppur, there was nothing left to do but swear and wait for better weather, or hope for a daring bus driver.

From now on I was to use this means of transportation to get to school. It became something like an airlock between two worlds, one of which—Kleppur—I viewed as my own and that people in the other one—the world outside Kleppur—thought was crazy. It always seemed to me that this should be exactly the reverse.

The people from Kleppur who traveled by bus to the city behaved a little strangely during the trip. They dressed differently, often in so-called fine clothes referred to as *Spariföt* (best clothes) because they were usually kept in the closet to be used for better occasions. When the weather was normal—that meant bad weather—waiting for the bus wasn't good for the clothes. There was no such thing as a covered bus stop. With a loud pop, umbrellas changed immediately into rain funnels, since rain in Iceland usually blows up from down below. One day someone came up with a promising invention: an umbrella with a see-through extension that reached to the ground. The fortunate possessor of such a rubberized cell was protected on all sides from the wind and the rain—at least that is what the inventor thought. What the inventor did not think of was protecting the owner from the protection itself. The wind simply blew the thin plastic surface along, and it didn't matter where the wind was coming from. Regardless, it blew between the owner's legs and feet, and his only choice was to try to stand firmly where he was or be helplessly blown over. Moving forward was not one of the choices. It actually got even worse when the storm blew the umbrella into the face of its carrier—into his mouth, nose, and eyes—and thus he was unable to carry anything since he had to use his other hand to protect himself.

This battle with the plastic tube—much to my regret—could be observed only for a few weeks. Gradually everyone realized that they had to look for something better. The solution was very original: it was called *Leigubifreið* (rental car), otherwise known as a taxi.

To get to my new school, the bus traveled only about ten minutes, but they were minutes filled with discoveries and temptations. Mostly I was taken by the swimming pool, which the bus rode past every day. From the outside there wasn't much to see, because the pool was surrounded by a man-high corrugated wall, but there was steam rising promisingly up into the air. I could see children of many ages going in, all happily laughing, with colorful towels rolled up and clasped under their arms. At school everybody spoke in the most tempting terms about swimming.

It did not remain a secret to my mother that I was interested in learning to swim. Probably she even realized that it might make her worries less in regard to my notoriously daring brother by knowing that we wouldn't automatically sink to the bottom if we fell into the ocean. In any case she registered us for swimming lessons at Sundlaug, but my brother was not exactly enthusiastic. He probably thought that anything someone else could teach him he could learn better by himself. On the other hand, I had great hopes and looked forward to the joys of the water about which I had heard so much in school.

The first day of swimming lessons was truly an impressive experience. Right inside the entranceway, I was fascinated by two things: the smell and the cashier. The anteroom to the pool was wrapped by a mysterious darkness. It smelled strongly of wood, soap, and sulfur, and maybe also a little bit of humanity. From every direction came the sounds of squeaking floorboards and banging doors. But I was most impressed by the cashier who peered with bugged-out and swollen eyes from a brightly lit little booth, like a fish peeking out from an aquarium, looking at the visitors and taking their money. We were registered for swimming lessons, but we were first required to undergo a test of our ability with the pool itself.

The usual equipment for student swimmers was put on us, but that led to considerable resistance by my brother. This time I could understand why, because the swimming coach was not exactly timid. Icelandic swimming students were always kept above water by an unusual float which bore a remarkable resemblance to the previously mentioned and indescribable rubber shoes. Most likely they both were made from the same automobile inner tubes.

From each inner tube they could make several pairs of shoes, but only one swim float.

This was the case because each tire had to have a valve. It stuck out like some kind of antenna from the swim float. To the right and to the left of the valve someone had cut the tube and sealed up the open ends.

Missing at this point was merely a strap to connect the float to a child. This was also made from tire rubber and attached firmly to the float.

The swimming coach looked for a float that would fit me, placed it on my back, and pulled the strap two or three times to make sure it was the right size. Each time he gleefully let it snap back, which I really didn't appreciate.

In my brother's case, his safety measures met with even less understanding. Probably he had already decided to himself that he would reject the services of the swimming coach.

The coach then put a flat piece of cork the size and shape of a book in our hands, and off we went to the water. I bravely climbed into the steaming brew, but my little brother did what I really wanted to do. He threw the piece of cork in the corner and ran over to the little spectator's balcony where our mother was waiting for things to get under way. He swiftly jumped over the railing. The swimming coach just shrugged his shoulders; it was just a trial lesson.

I was put in with a group of boys, and every week we had to practice froglike leg movements in the shallow part of the pool, pushing the cork along in front of us through the water. The bottom was slippery, and the water smelled and tasted like sulfur. The float on my back scratched and the strap pinched. These could not be the pleasures that the others had raved about.

Finally it had come to the point that I could take off the cursed float and leave the cork behind. Along with my classmates, I discovered the real joys that Sundlaug had to offer. That did not consist of swimming, but rather in not-swimming—more precisely, in doing nothing, and for that there was a shallow basin with especially hot water. The children lay in it like sardines, enjoying the pure warmth, and especially on those cold days when the icy wind blew around in the pool area.

Swimming pool with sun bathing area in the background

Another pleasure that was kept secret, especially by the older boys, I couldn't yet participate in. It had to do with two special sections of the pool site that were entered through two different doors that were always carefully kept shut. Women went through one of the doors and men through the other, both only on sunny days, of course. My schoolmates enlightened me. It was a place for sunbathers, and they were stark naked. That didn't interest me, but the others found that to be exciting and invited me to sneak around the pool with them, to holes in the wooden and tin fence that they ostensibly had found but probably had made themselves. I wasn't really comfortable with all this, but I was already enough of an outsider, and didn't want to call more attention to myself.

We got to the peepholes undetected, and I looked at some rather shapeless people who lay out in the sun. For the life of me, I couldn't find anything of interest. Baths in the section where my mother was in charge were much more exciting, most especially when the fattest woman with the unusual name of Bolla took her turn. Bolla had to be rolled over regularly in her bed, and from time to time she also had to be bathed. Several orderlies helped, and with a heave-ho she was lifted onto a gurney, pushed into the bathroom, and rolled into a bathtub already prepared for her. The only person who enjoyed this process was Bolla; she loved the bath, even when not much water was left in the tub after she had been pushed in with a splash.

I was suspicious that my comrades were a little screwy, the way they fought with each other for a look through the peephole. My doubts were even greater when I too got the chance to look through the hole at the people inside. For one thing, the sun didn't seem to have had any effect on the exterior of those who were sunbathing; they were just as pale as those who just went swimming. In spite of this, they were really keen on exposing every part of their body to the sun's rays. This went as far as bringing matches with them, which they cut into small pieces and wedged between their toes. The purpose was clearly to spread the toes apart in order to expose the hidden spaces to the wan sunlight.

The boys stood in something like a small swamp around the peephole, pushing repeatedly against the corrugated fence and, in the meantime, forgot to whisper. It was soon clear to me that the sunbathers knew about what was transpiring beyond the privacy wall, and their modesty boundary. Maybe they didn't care, and maybe they just allowed the boys to have their fun. Maybe too they just enjoyed all the fuss that was being made about their naked bodies and the attention the boys were so carefully devoting to the viewing. In any case, I had seen enough to know that I had seen enough.

It may also have played a role that I was being armed mightily as a WEBELOS—that is, as a fledgling Boy Scout.

My mother probably thought that it would be good for me to learn some discipline and, alongside the many crazies in the hospital to have some normal and well-mannered young boys around me. I didn't really feel this was necessary, but I went along with her wishes and made my way every Wednesday to the Boy Scout den. This was twice as far from Kleppur as the boarding school and was right in the middle of the city. I had to get off the bus at a mysterious and bad-smelling gas station on *Rotflussplatz* (Red River Square) even though there was no river to be seen far and wide. The previous stop was called *Ás* (Out), and everyone said that authority-respecting German tourists always obediently got off there. I didn't feel like that applied to me.

The Boy Scout den was housed in American barracks, which were found everywhere and made the city quite ugly. It was said, however, that they were more comfortable than the huts that one had to deal with earlier. The barracks looked like giant half sunken, rusted, and corrugated tin tubes. Inside they were not quite as ugly as they were on the outside. All things considered, it would not mean much in the way of damage if they were subjected to a direct hit by some enemy.

American barracks

The barracks for the Boy Scouts were decorated with hand-carved and amusingly painted totem poles, and there were comfortable chairs for members of the upper class. This consisted of the Boy Scouts themselves, who could be recognized by their brown shirts, which really didn't sit well with me. As a fledgling Scout rather than a brown shirt, I got a dark blue sweater with a little badge that was supposed to be a wolf, but I thought it looked more like a dog. I was not at all happy with such costuming, simply because I had mixed memories about uniforms.

March of Icelandic Boy Scouts

My activity as a Boy Scout consisted of studying for various tests, listening to stories, and memorizing proverbs and sayings. In my mind none of this made sense. Why should I learn to tie twenty different knots or find my way around in the outdoors with a compass in my hands and a blanket over my head? Exercises of this kind were life-threatening around Kleppur because of the cliffs, which caused the patients to trust their eyes even less than they normally would. After each successful test, a new badge was sewn onto the sweater.

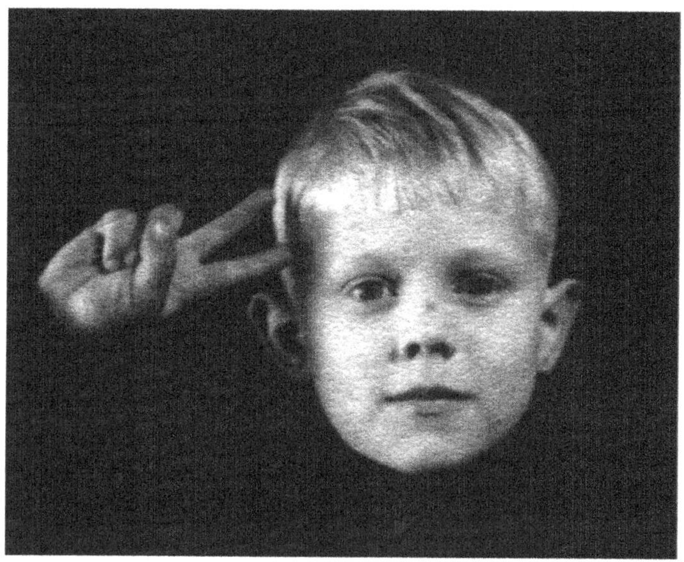

Cub Scout

At scout meetings and events I heard many stories, mostly about a great English general named Bipi, but that didn't seem to be a worthy name for such a brave man. He seems to have been very successful in training English boys in tracking down Dutch farmers in Africa. Strange and far-fetched, this seemed to me. Nevertheless, some impressions and values remained in my childish mind, thoughts which I later recognized when I had to change to the Catholic school in Landakot, run by Dutch priests and nuns.

To be sure, I was less than impressed by the wise sayings and well-intentioned proverbs that I took home with me every Wednesday; for example, the saying that one should do some good deed every day. In my ears that sounded like pure nonsense: one good deed and the rest of the day didn't matter. Once one has done a good deed, then for the rest of the day you can do or not do whatever you want to. Could one do some good deeds in advance and then be left in peace for several days? They gave us clear examples of all kinds of good deeds. One favorite and very special good deed was to help old people cross the street. In light of the street situation in Iceland, the example was difficult to understand, since the landscape on both sides of the street was much more difficult for old people to navigate than were the streets themselves. I thought that it might be a good deed to let a fledgling Scout help me cross the street so that he could fulfill his daily duty and in this way rise to the level of a full Boy Scout. Fledglings could thus help each other and in this way carry out a lot of good deeds in the shortest period of time.

The saying "learning by doing" seemed to me to be really unrealistic: you just had to firmly believe in success, we were told, then you can do anything. If that were actually the case—and many in the insane asylum truly believed it—then one should be able to fly. If you believed it enough, then you might jump headfirst out of the window and without hesitation. But how were you to know if your belief was strong enough to be able to leap? Assurance came only when you knew that you had already jumped!

First I jumped out of the window and landed hard, down below in the flower garden; and I learned at this point that I really couldn't fly or that my belief that I could fly wasn't really strong enough. You first had to learn how to believe, simply by believing, but then there was nothing more to learn! I decided at that point to no longer devote myself to such wild thought processes.

CHAPTER SIX

The Better Belief

Learning to believe was soon to play an important role in my life. It was, of course, not simply a matter of whether or how one believes, but rather what one believes, or especially, which church one went to on Sunday. Up until now it was completely unimportant; more precisely, I had something else in mind, as did my mother. That was, however, not the case with my relatives in far-off Bavaria. In their view I had fallen into the hands of the enemy and was being subjected to a deceitful, Protestant-Lutheran brainwashing.

I had actually not given any thought to why one goes to church, not even why churches are built.

The meaning of religious instruction had been made up solely in the little Bible pictures that we received at the conclusion of each hour of instruction. From regular contact with my many more or less quite different and crazy friends, I had become very practiced not in weighing the verbal expressions individually, but in viewing them as supportive of spiritual uniqueness. I had even developed an ambition to think my way into the abnormal and bizarre individual worlds of certain patients and to communicate with them. I was also quite successful—with few problems—in understanding the world of the religion teacher, but I didn't really find this very thrilling. Soon I could formulate sentences that he understood even if he wasn't particularly enthusiastic about them. I liked the praise and would have gotten into the scene even more, but then the firebomb letter arrived from Germany.

Far away, in Catholic Bavaria, nobody had spent much time thinking about the consequences of changing schools, not to mention churches in Reykjavik. For the relatives back there, the salvation of my soul obscured their senses, and my mother had no choice but to register me for the Catholic school at the other end of the city. She wasn't asked for her opinion, nor was I.

I was stinking mad on account of the Bible pictures, but she did not seem to notice. She didn't even try to explain to me this distant steering of my life, over land and sea, nor even to make it understandable why this abrupt change of school and confession was necessary. That was her way of making it clear to me that she was not in agreement. She became something of a mystery, and I began to ponder just what her religious world was like. It didn't seem to matter to her whether I attended Protestant religious education classes and learned there that the Catholics were on the wrong path to heaven, or whether I heard exactly the opposite from the Catholics. It soon became very clear to me that both knew about heaven and hell, the main difference being that for one group it was the Catholics—and for the other, the Protestants—who were roasting in hell, while each one enjoyed in full measure the luxury of heaven.

I must say, however, that the presentation of heaven and hell in the Bible pictures left a lasting impression on me. I simply could not get it in my head that the comforting warmth of fire should serve to torture villains. On the other hand, in heaven the blessed ones seemed to be only scantily clad, standing around pale-faced and freezing on icebergs. It was of no use to ask my mother about such suspect inconsistencies. The most one could get from her was "That's what they say." That sounded like she intended to say, "They just don't know any better." Her prayer probably said, "Lord, forgive them for they know not what they say." Most likely she would also not have said "Lord," but rather a quick and simple "I forgive them; they are trying to do their best, even if they appear to be so idiotic."

School in Landakot (Teachers' house on the right and behind it the gymnasium)

Thus intellectually and spiritually armed, I was taken by my mother at the beginning of my third year in school to Landakot. The bus only went to Lækjatorg, the hub of public transportation in Reykjavik, and from there we had to go by foot up the hill to where the Catholics resided. There they had a large meadow, a big hospital, and two churches, one old and one new. The old one had been turned into a gymnasium decades ago and moved around behind the schoolhouse. Here I was to spend the rest of my school years. The school building pleased me straight off; it reminded me of the architectural style out in the countryside—it seemed familiar, peaceful, and modest. Maybe someone even thought they might be able to use the school building as a church; they had built a bell tower that looked like a steeple.

The new church, however, was something of an architectural contrast, a kind of weapon in the religious wars, a poke in the eyes of the Protestants. The strike against their confessional opponents worked quite successfully. For anyone who arrived by sea in Reykjavik, which everybody did at that time, the first thing the eye saw was the proud but dark church rising like a throne over the city. The Catholic church thus became a symbol in a predominantly Protestant Reykjavik. At the same time, the recreated Gothic building style suggested foreign influence.

It was a German bishop—the Icelandic Catholics hadn't yet produced one—who had the church built. The Icelandic architect—a Protestant, of course—may have tried to insinuate himself into a Catholic-architectural sensitivity. In any case, the result is at best a huge, concrete misunderstanding, and in the worst case, a chess move in the enduring haggling of the confessions. Nevertheless, there is something moving about the structure, something like when one develops pity for a cripple or for someone on whom one has played a bad trick. It even appears that the lay bishop-architect felt this way too, by trying to make good on his building sin by putting rock crystal in the mortar. The church, according to his plan, was supposed to sparkle over the city like a celestial diamond when the sun was shining.

What he didn't think about was that raindrops also blink and flash in the sunlight, making the church look wet even in a dry storm. In that way one could say the church is very Icelandic.

The Protestants didn't leave this challenge unanswered, and they called on their most capable architects to plan an impressive counter-church on a second hill in the city. Higher and bigger, of course, but especially more Icelandic than the Catholic church. The main architect took up the task and sketched out such a magnificent church that only the plinth of the apsis could be financed. What was built was a semicircular bungalow-like church, which actually proved to be big enough for the congregation for many years. Not until much later, when there was more money in the country, was the building completed, and behold, there is nothing like it anywhere in the entire world! When looking at this church one thinks instinctively of a sea lion at the circus whose ball has just been taken from its nose. The flipper-fins resemble lightly curved basalt columns and grow on the sea hound or sea lion like a long mane all the way up to the head. In contrast to the Catholic church, the Protestant church is bright, almost white.

There is no such thing as white basalt columns, but it is said that belief can move mountains; can't it at least change the color in a little stone?

Thoughts of this kind were very far off for me on my first visit to Landakot, as one might imagine. I thought much more about the bad teeth of the rector of the school. In his surroundings there was a distinct smell, strong and unpleasant. Among the Protestants I had learned a lot about the incense burning of the Catholics, and their despicable smell. That must be true, I thought, and I tried to hold my breath for as long as possible.

Rector

My mother, of course, noticed my unnatural way of speaking, but the rector, with the aspirated or otherwise difficult-to-pronounce name Ubaghs, didn't bother her. Children in his presence often acted up, but much more likely, he traced my speech impediment back to the insane asylum. Aside from the smell, the rector was very congenial, and he probably saw in me one of the few truly Catholic children in the school. The majority, I soon found out, were indeed Protestants, like almost all Icelanders, but they went to the Catholic school because this was the only special school in the country, and there were always people who preferred something special over the usual. You learned about the same, and in about the same way, as in any other school, but it was really important that no one knew this.

In my case the situation was just the opposite. In far-off Bavaria there were people who were very worried whether what I was learning as the true belief was really and exactly the same as what they would have taught me in Bavaria if I had remained there. They wanted everything, but for God's sake nothing special. I didn't protest, and my mother, the Protestant, didn't either. I thought of only one thing—and my mother thought just as I did—how could we pacify the Bavarian relatives in the quickest and most effective way. She did not concern herself with what I believed or didn't believe, I think. She probably thought (and in this she was right) that I felt it was right to decide for myself what I believed and what I didn't believe.

What really stood out at school was a very corpulent German nun named Henrietta. She taught mathematics, and as a symbol of her profession she almost always had a ruler in her hand—a little like the Vikings once held their swords.

She also used the ruler as a weapon when she was of the opinion that it was needed to enforce a belief or prove a mathematical point. Always for the good of the students, of course! At the core of math instruction was multiplication, which one was to commit to memory, just like the Ten Commandments.

Henritta tried to funnel the multiplication tables into us, memorizing them the way we did with poetry. She had apparently had the experience that Icelanders were very receptive to this didactic methodology, but that wasn't quite the case with me. I didn't want to repeat prayer-like these sinewy litanies. The story about null seemed very suspicious to me. Why was null times null always null? I even dared one time to ask our fat nun this question, but I knew right away that I should not have done that. She looked at me with precisely the same look that the patients in Kleppur did when I succeeded in interrupting them from having the same thought, and causing them for a moment to be torn from their safe world in their safe routine. Her mouth hung open and formed a little circle on the larger circle of her face. I was expecting the worst, since the ruler in her fat hand threatened havoc. I heard a deep and angry sound coming from her mouth: Oooo…, it sounded like a volcano was about to erupt, and every Icelander knows what that means.

But it really wasn't as bad as I thought it might be, and she just said: "That's the way it is." Somehow I had the feeling that I had emerged as victor in an intellectual duel. The pleasure didn't last long, however, since I had really given Henrietta the bird. It was good that the incident happened near the end of the school year and the next year began with a new teacher. She too was a cloister nun, but of a very different type. In contrast to Henrietta, she was not German but Icelandic, small and thin as a rake. What she was lacking in body mass she made up for in energy. Her previous Icelandic name was Svanlaug, which could be roughly translated as "swan's bath," and stood in stark contrast to her outwardly resolute, not to mention self-confident, authoritarian and yet antiauthoritarian appearance.

The cloister name chosen for her was Clementia, which meant something like "the lenient one." Icelanders turned that into "Klemma," which is related to the German word *Klemme* (hair clip) and outwardly fit her character. She seemed to be completely in control of everything, but in fact she was quite helter-skelter in her actions.

She got into a jam with—at that time, anyway—the quite-lenient traffic police in Reykjavik, since she really liked to drive the cloister delivery truck into town. However, she didn't pay attention to the road signs and the traffic rules, seeing them merely as suggestions and not as prescriptions on how one was to behave in traffic. Such behavior was at the time not unusual for Icelanders. Someone later explained to me that traffic lights served the purpose only of deciding who was guilty when there were accidents. Klemma, in any case, drove the way she wanted to, like a thoroughly guilt-free cloister nun married to Jesus, and people got used to her and simply got out of her way.

I got to know two of the teachers at Landakot quite well, or, better said, they got to know me. Hákon, the religion and Danish teacher, had gone to school with my half-brother Leo in Akureyri. Guðún frá Skál came from my rural home in Síða. In German, what sounds like she came from nobility simply means in Icelandic that she came from the farm of Skál. It was something like the poorest of the poor farms in that area, and it was in the same area where my grandparents lived; their farm won out in poorness over my grandparents' farm in Heiðarsel, and Skál was even more difficult to get to. Back then no automobile had ever made it to my grandparents, at least not to our farm. The trip on horseback lasted several hours, after which I could not sit without pain for several days.

Guðún taught Icelandic and history, and in such an inspired way that I immediately decided to become a writer. There was also the fact that we were distant relatives, so much so that I could at least imagine that a talent for storytelling was also slumbering somewhere within me.

Guðún frá Skál

History instruction consisted mostly of telling stories; one could even say, somewhat disrespectfully, of reciting sagas. Guðún had mastered them absolutely. One even had the impression that she just sat there and with no difficulty told about something that she had just experienced a short time before. It was inconceivable that she had not been there, and we were all amazed when the warrior Viking Egill could not psychically deal with his defeat in ice hockey and continued the game raging mad with an axe and split open the skulls of his opponents.

His father, Gímur the Bald, acted the same way when Egill defeated him. It was only through the intervention of a slave woman that Egill came away with his life. For this the father then drowned the slave.

As scholars later learned, Egill would not have to fear blows to his head, for his skull bone did not stop growing like that of other people, remaining thin and fragile. Rather, it kept growing until it was thick and resistant, like a helmet grafted onto his head.

Sword blows to his head could barely hurt Egill. The sword of his opponent stuck in his skull, and with great ease Egill then sent his stunned and quickly beheaded rival to Valhalla. We can assume that his skull bone grew outward, not inward. He had mastered poetry while he was still in the cradle, and it is said that at the age of three he was already composing and reciting poetry. Later, then, when he didn't have anything to chop up, he hired out as a *Scald* (singer of poetry) and sang unusually elaborate songs of praise to the Norwegian king Erik, who bore the threatening epithet Bloodaxe. Erik's wife Gunnhildur was not impressed by Egill's thick skull, and for whatever reason set him free after Bloodaxe had come to grief. From this point on, Egill had to kill off his troublesome followers, but soon tired of that and returned to Iceland. There he was depressed when two of his sons were prematurely sent off to Valhalla, and then he became preoccupied with following them there. For that he needed sufficient power over offended or angered opponents, but it was never that difficult to find them. The cheapest and most effective method of fatally insulting someone was to chop off the head of a horse, putting it up on a stake, and planting it in the garden of an enemy. In some cases the procedure brought on trouble, since Egill's older son had died in a storm brought on by the sea god Ægir and his wife Rán.

The warrior then fell deeper into depression, and in an act of utter confusion crawled back into his bed, refused sustenance, and waited for an inglorious deathbed trip to the underworld.

The planned end of the story for Egill was interrupted by a seemingly modern act of crisis intervention. His daughter, Þorgerður, who seemed to have a psycho-therapeutical and natural gift, laid down in the bed with her father, and like a saint said that she wanted to die with him. The father didn't care, and so they lay and waited for death together. Such waiting can be very boring, and so the daughter whiled away the time chewing on seaweed. To be more precise, this was a special kind of seaweed, called "*söl*" (salt), suggestive of salt taste and the salad that it looked like—in addition, of course, to the seaweed taste. Off and on, Þorgerður gave her father a little bit to chew on. The effect was soon apparent: her father was overcome by a terrible thirst and a real Viking can neither live nor die this way. So, drinks were offered, and cleverly not water but milk. Egill drank the way he always had, and death was out of the picture for a while. In order not to waste this miraculous revival, Egill decided to seize the opportunity for poetic inspiration, creating an impressive and expressive poem about the frustration, sadness, and rage in his soul.

Guðrúns students listened to stories like this as if they were crime novels. Her Saga-hours were so popular that she even included them on non-school day afternoons, and not a single student was absent. I just couldn't get it into my head that Guðrún had memorized all of these stories. Maybe, I thought, she just knew the basic series of the historical events and made up the rest. On the other hand, I knew that the Icelanders at that time were second to none in committing stories to memory. For hours on end they could recite poems, indeed they even had competitions where the winner was the one who knew the most poems. In olden times, during the cold winters, my mother told me that the children liked to sit together in the nearly dark *Baðsstofa* [sitting room], the combination bedroom and living area of the traditional Icelandic farmhouse, and recite the entire array of poems. The next teller always had to begin his poem with the same letter that the previous storyteller had ended his account. It was absolutely forbidden the repeat a poem.

Sittings like this could go on for hours, and some even had to be adjourned. My mother was mostly the winner at such competitions and had accordingly acquired the pseudonym *Vísnatobba*. *Vísa* (stanza) has the meaning of a "short poem," and *Tobba* was her nickname. She also liked to tell the story of her confirmation lessons, which consisted of distributing four Psalm books to twelve children being confirmed. Every child then had three months to commit the psalms to memory. The cleverest children got to keep the books because they had remembered the entire 150 psalms for the longest time, eight months. It was said of Icelandic students in Copenhagen that they could recite an entire Danish newspaper after reading it just one time.

Maybe Guðrún had in fact committed all of the saga texts to memory, or at least mostly so. This idea would not leave me alone, and so I decided to pursue the matter. For this purpose I borrowed from the head nun Guðríður the volume with the saga that Guðrún was going to recite, and I tried to follow her presentation word for word. It wasn't as simple as I thought it would be. Just when I had found one sentence, the next one followed and caused confusion for me. I tried to make notes for myself, but I wasn't fast enough with my writing and forgot the passage while recording it. Guðrún also had the habit of continuing to babble between the words of the saga. I was frustrated, and after school went home with only a couple of unreliable parts of sentences, and set about making comparisons. I actually found those portions of the text that I had written down, but then my memory faded. It soon seemed to me that what was in the book was only a shorter version of what Guðrún had been telling us. In my head her story took on more and more the nature of the original, and so I began to ask if perhaps Guðrún's story wasn't in fact closer to the actual happenings than the narrative of someone who had done a thousand years ago exactly what Guðrún had just done, namely breathe life into the stories already in the heads of the listeners.

The story played out in a believable form in her head, and in her narrative she presented it to us as if it was being told at the original location of the happening.

Egill Skallagrimsson really did it to me, because all of the Helgis who were in the Edda were without exception not especially good role models for me. One was named Helgi the Thin; he was married to a woman with the name Þórunn the Horned, and her father was called Ketill Flatnose. Another Helgi, Helgi Hjörvarðssib, was not given a name when he was a child because he refused to speak and, according to the belief at that time, he had no soul. He got his name during his years as a youth. He was sitting silently, as always, on a grave mound when nine Valkyries rode up on their flying horses. One of the Valkyries named Sváfa spoke to him and gave him the name Helgi. She then told him that if he continued to hold his tongue he would never accomplish anything in life. Now, freshly baptized and animated, Helgi understood this, and wanted to marry the Valkyrie right away. Only then would he be ready to accept her baptismal gift, an especially sharp sword. The marriage didn't come until much later, but Sváfa hovered from this point on over Helgi and protected him. When reading this, I learned that the name Helgi was not as I had previously thought, associated with Sunday and holidays, that in Icelandic are called *helgidagar* (holy days). Rather, it means the "Holy one," not in the Christian sense but in the Viking sense, and was reserved by them for princes and heroes.

A third Helgi, Helgi Hundingsbani, was a precocious murderer and was able to take revenge for his father. At the delicate age of fifteen he did Hunding in, the man who had slain his father. He was later to become an opera star in a Richard Wagner opera. This Helgi also met a Valkyrie, Sigrún, who was just about to be married off by her father in an arranged marriage. Helgi helped her out of this situation by quickly killing off the entire family. He had mercy on a brother named Dagur, and left him alive—as a warning to every Viking. Dagur swore in the name of Odin to take revenge, and Odin, who had a weakness for those who sought revenge, lent him his super spear. Helgi didn't have a chance against it, and Dagur told his sister about his heroic deed. She was not at all impressed by this and cursed her brother, and from this day forward he stumbled from one misfortune into another.

Now the story gets interesting. Helgi was able to sneak out of Valhalla for one night and to spend that same night with Sigrún on his own grave mound. However, he had to be back in Valhalla by dawn because the household rooster woke up the Einherja, the dead warriors, who immediately set out to spend the entire day with their favorite pastime, killing each other off.

Odin then had some pangs of conscience and offered Helgi a place of honor at his side in Valhalla, and later, after Sigrún had died, granted both of them a veritable rebirth. Before this happened, however, Helgi used his elevated status in Valhalla to demote his former opponent, the once-mighty Viking king Hunding, to herding swine, feeding dogs, and washing feet.

I believed every word by Guðrún, as much as I believed anybody, since anyone growing up in an insane asylum develops a special kind of gullibility. There one hears many strange and not-so-strange, believable and unbelievable, stories. You listen to them and believe that the one who is talking also believes what is being said. Just how that could be is of no real importance. Maybe they are all wrong—after all, they are insane—but maybe none of them is wrong, they just express themselves differently. Among Icelanders that has a long tradition, to say the same thing in a different way—it is called poetic license. If you learn something by heart, that's not so that you know something; rather it is so that you can listen to yourself and then think about it for a while.

Here was Egill grieving for his sons to the point that he no longer wanted to die the death of a hero. Instead he decided on a hunger strike, and then, at the end, feared what was called "grass" death—dying in bed—which meant nothing less than that being denied entry to Valhalla, and thus the joyous daily bloodbath with the other warriors. Egill was at odds with Odin, who himself had lost his son Baldur to a trick by the arch scoundrel and anti-god Loki. Somehow that all sounded familiar to me, from religious instruction. God's son was betrayed and hanged on the cross, Abraham was on the verge of sacrificing his own son on the orders of God. It seemed to be repeated over and over again, this way or that way, sometimes more, sometimes less colorful in the words used to describe the situation. All were concerned about the future that bound them to their oldest or perhaps only son. The son represented their living on even after death, for how it proceeds and how it continues: it meant life.

The old Icelanders were in any case masters at the art of description, one could also say at beating around the bush. To simply call something by its name offered no satisfaction to them. The Valkyries became for them the daughters of heaven or the wind, even when their biological father was well known. The waves were for them the daughters of the sea, or of a sea god, even if no one knew how the gods procreated. For Christians, the demons and many evil people are spawned in hell or in darkness, or are even the sons of Satan. Whether someone meant such name calling in earnest, that remained up to him, but I had learned from my mother never to ask such questions.

She never had the idea to try to convince a patient that it was a mistake to think of himself as Jesus, a prophet, a spokesman for God, or even God himself. She would have understood him, without taking his words for the truth. The most unusual thing was that she seemed to understand those under her care, and did not think about what they were trying to say. To understand was for her something like direct bonding—maybe love of mankind would be a better phrase—with what was happening. It only came to me much, much later that I must have drunk this in, quasi, from my mother's milk, not reasoned it out. My Bavarian relatives, including my father, had no premonition what a winding road—as seen by them—I had set out on.

Perhaps they actually saw something more troublesome, for one day it was explained to me that I had to undergo a special Catholic religious treatment. It was explained to me as necessary preparation for my first communion, which actually wasn't scheduled for another year, and didn't really mean much to me. Because there were so few students, the instruction had to be carried out on an individual basis. For my teacher, Hákon Loftsson was chosen, the only Catholic priest in Iceland. The instruction took place at the bishop's house in a street named Egillsgata, a name that only somewhat appeased me in regard to what was to transpire there. From now on I had to find my way there every two weeks for religious instruction.

Hákon the religion teacher

Hákon turned out to be exceptionally courteous and surely sensed that my enthusiasm for religious matters was very limited. It was helpful that he knew my half-brother Leo, whom my father had sent to school in Akureyri in north Iceland before the war. It was father's hope that he would be able to keep Leo away from the growing Hitler mania in Germany. Hákon, however, could make little headway with me, in spite of such family ties. I accepted my fate, more or less, and played the game as best I could. Sometimes I had real difficulty with pretending, for example when Hákon and Bishop Jóhannes tried to reward me for exceptional learning accomplishments with warm honey-milk. They themselves never touched the stuff.

They had a little more success in teaching me when they came upon the idea of establishing personal contact for me with a truly supernatural being, at least in my eyes; namely, Tarzan, the king of the jungle. In the beginning I viewed the promise as a rather obvious trick, but Hákon, it turned out, had indeed rather personal contacts with Hollywood.

Hákon's father was the leading photographer in Reykjavik, a lucrative situation since it was considered good taste to photograph children every couple of years, for the future. My brother and I were mercilessly subjected to this ritual: first a cleansing bath and then being forced into uncomfortable and increasingly tighter Sunday clothes. Our hair had to be cut and, in my case, protruding ears pressed with skin-colored bandages to my head, and finally to smile in a friendly way while posing before the camera: really a horror!

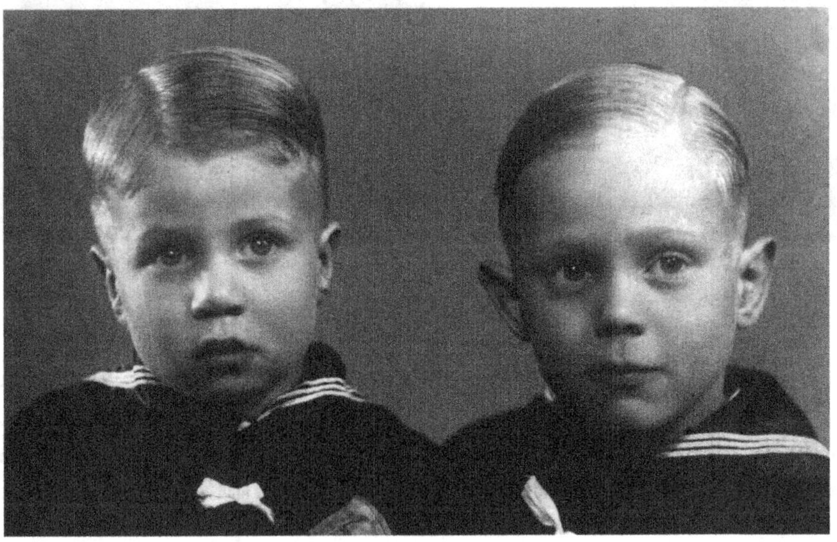

Obligatory annual photo

Hákon's well respected and strictly Protestant family was in turmoil when their offspring showed a clear interest in Catholic mass ceremonies and decided not only to convert to Catholicism but also to study and become a priest. The family was, to be sure,

Icelandic, and open enough to not stand in the way of his wishes, and so they sent the boy to America, to a priest seminary somewhere near Boston—from an Icelandic viewpoint close to Los Angeles.

At the same time, Americans had messed things up in Hollywood with their film technology, and had developed cameras that were recording both sound and image at the same time. What they had not thought about was that the cameras didn't just record the sound that was part of the film, but every other sound, including the humming noise made by the camera itself. They tried to take care of this by insulating the cameras, but this increased their size horribly. Then they were confused because the film could not be spliced as easily as before. The sound and the image were at different places on the film, and so the jerking motion of the film when the image advanced presented audiences with garbled language.

In brief, they decided to scrap the cameras. Hákon's father, Loftur, got wind of this and saw the chance to advance his chances from the best photographer in Iceland to the first filmmaker in Iceland. Background noise, he thought, does not exist in Iceland. He showed his interest by purchasing a monster-sized camera. This apparently caused the gentlemen in Hollywood to have a bad conscience, and they probably thought that the Eskimo over there had no idea what he was doing to himself. In order to clear their conscience, they offered, as something of an add on gift, to train a sound engineer on working with the complicated cameras. Loftur didn't really have an engineer, but he had a son in the priest seminary not too far away from Hollywood.

Hákon the priest was then placed on leave and set out for Hollywood, out to the Babel tower of sin. In Hollywood, Hákon learned a lot more than the art of making a talking film with the newly screwed-up camera technology. Above all, he got to know some of the famous great ones in the world of film; among them was exactly that Johnny Weissmüller, the best Tarzan actor in film history. It was his famous ape call, when he was placed in a nursing home, that awakened his slumbering fellow companions from their beds and drove the personnel crazy. This same Weissmüller wrote Hákon a letter, and I really couldn't believe my eyes when a personal letter from Tarzan, with a photo and his signature, arrived for me at Kleppur.

Johnny Weismüller

Another well-known figure, a man by the name of Marlon (Brando), called up on the telephone one day and wanted to speak with Hákon. It was obviously difficult for the priest and he seldom talked about those times, answering questions only indirectly. In the final analysis, it was a matter of religious instruction, and the bishop walked around lightly on the carpet, laughing in a friendly way and listening from the background.

This instruction was about truth, that was clear, not truth as such, not what one knew deep down inside, but what one learned by memory and what came primarily from the Pope. That is what I was taught to believe! I said yes, and amen, and thought back about those who told me that the truth was in the Bible, and about those individuals I was supposed to believe! I was able to understand both of them and what they had to say.

Naturally I also wanted to know if the Pope could tell a lie, just like everybody else (maybe even better), and just how he could be so sure that he was telling the truth. To questions of this sort I received nothing in return, which caused me to think out new provocative questions to try to get away from those sticky-sweet rewards. Hákon on the one hand seemed to find pleasure in my notorious disagreements, but on the other hand he felt that he was responsible that I did not stand out in religious circles.

The story about truth left me no peace. I had an acquaintance in the insane asylum who repeated again and again, day in and day out: "I am telling the truth, I am telling the truth, I am telling the truth." I was successful on several occasions to interrupt his monotonous flow of words by simply repeating what he was saying. I also said, "I am telling the truth, I am telling the truth ...." And so it happened that he was confused and stopped, he looked as if he had just risen from a deep sleep, was silent for a little while, and then said, "No, *I* am telling the truth!" Sometimes he interrupted and inserted asides, like "Well, and!" or "You don't say!" or simply with a pointed *un* thrown in precisely before the word *truth*.

I told my religion instructor about the truth-sayer at Kleppur and wanted to know if he wasn't actually telling the truth, since he never said anything other than that he was telling the truth. Hákon was of the opinion that the man was crazy and did not know what he was saying. Actually he didn't say anything; just repeated himself. He could have sung hallelujah all day long, or counted his fingers, he would have arrived at the same point!

The next point of contention was the human soul. I was of the opinion that there must be a mistake, since without a soul nobody needs anything; either one has one, or one doesn't need one. If indeed there was something like a soul, then it must go in and out of the body, just as I went in and out of Kleppur. Then my teacher looked at me in triumph and told me that in his personal experience that had actually happened. He had frequently climbed out of his body and had looked at it from the outside, as if he were hovering over himself, up near the ceiling of his room. It was a dream,

I thought, but it was unusual that it seemed to happen so regularly. Hákon maintained that he could sense when it was to the point that climbing out of his body was about to happen. We agreed to conduct an experiment that was to convince me once and for all about the Christian teaching about the soul. When he had the premonition, he was to go into an adjoining room and lie down on a couch. In the meantime, I was to make an obvious change of something in the room. If he could really leave his body, and as he maintained, move about freely, then he could briefly cast a glance into the room and see what I had done.

We were in luck; several weeks later, he had a premonition during class. He disappeared into the room next door, and I hung the bishop's hat on the chandelier. When Hákon came back after about half an hour, he was completely convinced that his soul had flown around the room. "Well, and what did you see?" I asked, "What did I do so that you would notice it?" His answer: "Nothing; you didn't do anything and probably were just trying to trick me." I told him about the bishop's hat and the chandelier, but he continued to say that there was nothing to see that was in some way noticeable. That was his truth, I was beginning to understand, and mine was the bishop's hat and the chandelier. I didn't have to think for a long time, the way my mother would have. She would have believed both of us, and that I decided was in fact the better belief, the belief that we were both convinced and wanted only the best. We were talking past each other and should rather find common ground. This unusual religious instruction came to a natural end in the form of Holy Communion. I had to appear, squeezed into a dark suit and half choked by a tie, in the dark church at Landakot, a memorable first public entrance. I was the only communion candidate this year and had scarcely any knowledge of church rituals. They had tried several times to recruit me for service in the church, but I had always succeeded in getting out of the assignment. The temptation to try it at least was enormous because the priest, named Josef Hacking, offered an entire unopened package of Wrigley's Juicy Fruit chewing gum as a reward.

It was a temptation that few of my friends at that time would have been able to resist, if they had been Catholic. I told Hacking that I would lead him to a couple of boys from my circle of friends who might be interested, but he was of the opinion that this was a service to God and thus Protestant boys weren't appropriate.

Hacking

Thus, I had to muddle my way through communion, with no experience in church matters. Hákon, my religion teacher, did give me exact instructions (when and where I had to go), but he was not convinced that I wouldn't do something crazy. So he hid behind a column and waved his instructions to me, which actually I could have interpreted as telling me to get out of there. It turned out that everything was much simpler than I had imagined, for just at that point in the liturgy the entire congregation stared expectantly at me and thus guided me with their eyes up to the altar. All of a sudden I felt very small and abandoned; the dark pseudo-Gothic columns rose up like gigantic pipes to heaven, and I was afraid that God's anger could come down through them and onto me. It was understandable; I had harbored every possible doubt and thought out the craziest things in regard to Him. All of this could certainly not have pleased Him. On the other hand, I thought, He could show his unending goodness toward someone who really needed it.

While I was thinking about these last matters and expected at any moment the worst to come down from above, I strolled like a sleepwalker between the women on the left and the men on the right, toward my inevitable fate. I actually reached the assigned place at the altar.

Out of the corner of my eye, I spotted Hákon standing behind the column, opening and closing his mouth, and I knew what he was trying to tell me. Then he grasped at his throat so as to tell me that I was supposed to swallow the dry piece of paperlike wafer that the bishop had placed in my mouth. Easier said than done. I thought, how nice for the Protestants, that they can disappear in the masses, and that on such occasions they even got something to drink.

CHAPTER SEVEN

The Better Language

Big happenings were in the works. Our father, so we heard, would soon come from Germany for a visit. He was one of the last to be released from the camp in Garmisch, simply because it proved to be difficult, and finally even impossible, to accuse him of being a supporter of the Third Reich. The news caused me to begin brooding again. How could anyone prove that he was not a criminal; couldn't one simply prove that all by himself? Was I perhaps a criminal because I didn't really think about whether I was one or not, or even now, because my thoughts about it were wrong? I asked some of my wiser friends from the insane asylum, but they just smiled politely as if such confusion of the mind was part of their everyday life. They wisely warned: you think too much; that is not healthy! That was no way to give me peace, since even not-thinking has to be practiced, just like keeping silent. Anyone who couldn't do that was damned to endless babbling and ended up in the restless ward of the asylum. Many of those in there talked incessantly about something that no one listened to, while day to day others repeatedly recited a poem or even a sentence. In the worst cases the brain spun around a single word, something like *Togari*. *Togari* is a German word for "a puller," a dragging puller, and that means a tugboat or trawler. The young man whose mind had mastered this word always sat, when he was allowed to, by an open window, staring out at the ocean, and, without stopping, repeated the word *Togari*. One time I was able to carry on a minimum of conversation with him, by repeating in rhythm with his *Togari* the word *tappa*. *Tappi* meant "plug," and the combination *Tappatogari* thus meant "cork screw." It took a little while, then he stopped his repetitions, but I couldn't get over the impression that he looked at me a little bit angered but much more relieved.

I had long since forgotten German, and when my father finally arrived in Reykjavik he spoke a strange incomprehensible and especially ugly language. That probably comes from the fact that Icelanders, in contrast to Germans, like to listen to the sound and the melody of their language. Germans are intent on saying something; Icelanders, on the other hand, want to hear something, even if it is only their own talking. Germans use their language; Icelanders play with theirs. In any case, I got this impression when I began to deal with the German language and the thoughts of my father. He was through and through a scholar and was searching like all scholars for the truth.

I had the feeling that he preferred to search around in the past, in that which had already happened, and not in what was happening now. The old Icelandic farmsteads had moved him, even though they were little more than simple mounds of dirt. He was interested in the language of Icelanders, especially because it was so old. That which was old was genuine, and it didn't seem to please him when I carefully expressed the opinion that the old had at one time also been new. Nevertheless, he always spoke about a living and continually developing language, and that one had to observe just how and to what extent it had developed. Only the spoken language was actually and really alive. When a language is set down, it is no longer a child of the human spirit, but rather its guardian. With writing, so I was to understand, humans lose out in intellectual freedom of expression. What is written—language that can be recorded—prescribes how we are to think.

Naturally I didn't think that way back then, but with the arrival of my father I began to think about natural language. He spoke German with my mother, which actually angered me because I couldn't understand what they were saying. With the two of us brothers he spoke Icelandic, and that seemed to me like punishment, even though I understood him completely. He spoke a kind of German-Icelandic, or better said, he used the Icelandic language in a German way.

My grandparents on the isolated farm almost never spoke because there was nothing to say. When they spoke, however, it was with the most beautiful and well-chosen words. Sometimes they just talked for no apparent reason and without really wanting to tell somebody something. They might just as well have sung a song, or whistled, but that was what Icelandic farmers did, at least those I got to know. Language served only partially to convey something to another person. They enjoyed speaking and playing with the language, and they would rather be silent than to fire off some inartistic blabbering. They played with their language like a musician playing with his instrument.

My father didn't play on the instrument of language; he took it apart and put it back together again; he researched it in order to reveal its secrets, how it had developed into what it is, but not to probe its possibilities or its boundaries. In secret, however, he did do this by composing numerous poems, which he then kept to himself. Creating poems was perhaps his kind of speaking with himself.

As a language researcher, there wasn't much for my father to do in Iceland, because the language hadn't changed much there since the time of the Vikings and the word acrobatics of the scalds. There is no such thing as dialects in Iceland, but when my father learned Icelandic he viewed it as a dialect—as a rather old Germanic dialect.

His well-known and feared thirst for action was suddenly subject to very narrow boundaries. Even in the Garmish camp he had organized theater plays, wrote several himself, and held lectures. But now his most important tool, the language, more precisely the German language, was almost completely removed from him.

In the beginning he spent his time with building activities. We were moved into a small settlement that had been built for the employees of the hospital. The settlement consisted of a row of small, white houses, low to the earth and containing two apartments each.

Nurses in front of the nurses' house

Two somewhat larger houses were reserved for new caretaker recruits who each were assigned one room. All of the nurses were particularly happy, even though under extreme wind conditions they had to make their way on all fours from the hospital to the little houses.

My father immediately thought about architectural enhancements. It was like a poke in the eye for him that the buildings lacked both cellars and attics; in other words, no place for storage. The nuns didn't really have anything to store and found his thoughts on the matter incomprehensible. My mother, however—how could it be otherwise—once again showed understanding and let him go on about his business.

As a fighter on the front during World War I my father knew how to dig out trenches, and so it didn't take long for him to dig out a veritable ditch behind the house, which he saw as a future earthen cave for potatoes and beets. Where he planned to acquire them was not known by anybody. It made me think that my father was making preparations for a third world war.

Hut in Summer

Hut in Winter

He was able to find the appropriate material for roof construction very easily. Thanks to the aforementioned wind conditions, it lay strewn all over the landscape. The building, when finished, fit harmoniously into the landscape, because it had long been the custom to allow patients from rural areas, perhaps with therapeutic thoughts, to build little earthen houses for themselves close to the hospital.

When the building was completed, my father then turned to growing food to eat. There was actually more than enough to eat, but he was somehow missing important ingredients and planned to get them through his own efforts. To begin with, he planted cucumbers in a box on the heater in the living-room window. He chose for this project a very productive small cucumber sort that climbed quite high and darkened our little living room.

He planned to put the cucumbers in vinegar and preserve them in the earthen cellar for future use. I have maintained my dislike of cucumbers in vinegar till this very day!

In the first postwar years in Germany, fruit played a very important role—first as a delicacy—and so my father thought that a hearty kind of apple would grow if it was planted next to the wall of the house and out of the wind. In some mysterious way he was able to acquire an apple seedling and planted it next to our house as an espalier tree. The tree actually survived, but refused to grow; I thought that it even shrank. When we left the house many years later, it was still that little needy sprig, and we left it for friends as a houseplant.

The apple tree

What my father intended to say with all of his activity—and this he could express in good Icelandic—was not the point. It's like food that is more than just sustenance.

In addition to the nutritive value, there is also the matter of enjoyment, and many people like foods that are not good for them. Taste is what matters for those who enjoy food. I think this aspect of the Icelandic culture was not easy for my father. He also, for example, did not participate in singing, but left that to others, and justifiably so.

Since he never reached the linguistic art of the Icelandic soul, he turned toward another art form, to painting. He did this with amazing energy and thoroughness. He bought paper and watercolors and began to paint, and he painted that which the Icelanders love almost as much as their language, their Icelandic landscape. As a scholar he obviously painted only what he saw (and, to be more precise, it wasn't much more than he could see from the window of his bedroom): the mountain overlooking Reykjavik, the Esja. He was not at all discouraged; instead, he painted this very impressive mountain in every lighting variation and every season. Soon we had piles of Esja pictures in the most varied formats. My mother did her best to give them to friends and relatives, and this artistic activity soon had the desired effect: my father was discovered by the Icelanders themselves, not as a linguist but as a painter of watercolors. I watched his behavior with amazement. Occupational therapy was something I understood, but in the hospital and under the direction of the beloved therapist Jóna, the patients didn't paint. Instead the men sawed, filed, and polished bones; women embroidered and knitted, depending on which level of calmness they found themselves in. The men produced mostly knives, as was fitting for retired Vikings; not weapons but rather dull letter openers. Following my Boy Scout's motto that one should begin right away with doing and not with learning, I tried out both disciplines. I had already produced a crooked and useless letter opener, so now I tried painting. Neither the process nor the result convinced me. My father said that I had "talent," but I thought that I could do without whatever that was.

Communication between father and son just didn't work out. He was just as strange to me as I was to him; we belonged to different worlds and spoke different languages. He just looked at me with resignation, and it only got worse when we received the news that Leo, my half-brother, his firstborn son, had died from complications of the war. All of my father's attempts to keep him away from the idiocy that had taken over the Germans was to no avail. He died of a lung infection. Antibiotics would probably have saved him, but they were not available in Germany for a few years to come.

My father seemed to be troubled about the scholarly inactivity to which he had been damned in Reykjavik. He was in body and soul a linguistics and folklore scholar, and his discipline was Germanics, especially dialect studies. Icelanders are, from their youth on, students of Old Germanic, and are more or less nimble language artists, but they have only heard about dialects.

Just when he reached this low point, I began to sense it and to understand him better. He came close to the abnormal normality that I was familiar with. Of course I thought about Egill and his son Böðvar, about Odin and Baldur, and I thought about how it must feel to speak a language that appealed only to their understanding, not to their feelings. It was like just exchanging numbers. And so finally we got into a conversation: a conversation about language.

He was of the opinion that I should learn German and go to a German school, but I was anything but convinced of this. I had already had problems with that unusual language, Danish. Danish was a required subject in Landakot, like swimming and gymnastics, but not as well liked. My religion teacher Hákon was also my Danish teacher, and contributed only very little to my enthusiasm for the language. It seemed to me that Danish, like Faroese, was nothing more than a twisted form of Icelandic. On the Faroe Islands, for example, they don't say sport teacher but body-trunk tamer, and earthquake is earth-crust shaking. Even worse, the Danes call the forehead a "frying pan," and while speaking make sounds that elsewhere would ban children from the table or send them to an internist. In general, the relationship between the Icelanders and the Danes appears to be some kind of confrontational attraction. On the one hand their deep friendship was publicly and continually alluded to, but on the other hand there were dogs running around in the countryside with names like Kong Frederik and Kong Christian.

My father thought that I would learn German in no time; after all, it was derived from Icelandic. I just had to learn a little language history, shift a few sounds, and learn a couple of new words that Germans had taken from somewhere else. He said it wasn't much different with English, and even though he had never studied it, he could understand it quite well. It was for him most interesting to learn those dead languages like Greek and Latin, and best of all was to add Hebrew and Hindustani to the list. Again I thought, he's nuts!

When he realized that he was not able to get my attention that way, he talked to me about the language of the future. In my ears, that at least sounded more reasonable. Since such a language did not yet exist, he created one. As I had always done, I did not doubt that he believed this, but I was even more confused when he told me more about his new language. He could even speak it, and had the feeling that he actually knew what he was saying.

This new language was called Pantal and was destined to become a world language. What fascinated me, however, was that he didn't really intend to invent it. It was supposed to invent itself, after a fashion. Like other languages it was also supposed to develop, just on a worldwide basis. That meant that every culture had the right to contribute to its growth, he just wanted to be the one who sewed the seed.

This still wasn't enough. He had developed a world-journal that was to aid in general understanding among the people, and in this way was intended to promote the development of Pantal throughout the world. The symbols were shaped in such a way that they would be understandable to everyone, worldwide, and that meant that they wouldn't have to learn the language first. I learned, in the futuristic language that for the time being only my father knew, that I was born on the tenfü-fü-taus-nun-tren-nu.

Crazy systems were familiar to me, and had even fascinated me ever since I had become acclimated to Kleppur. I had always been amazed at examples of lunacy—constructions and wild digressions of the mind, even if they were insane.

Gradually something was awakening inside me, like an interest in getting to know my father better and in learning languages. I was particularly interested in the possibility of understanding English-language films without having to learn English. Up to this point I had understood only silent movies, and I was angry that I could not grasp what Tarzan and Roy Rogers were saying. There were no films in which Icelandic was spoken, with only one small exception. It was the first and very unusual piece done by Hákon's father Loftur: *Síðasti bærinn í dalnum*, which in translation means "The Last Farm in the Valley." The film was intended for an uncritical audience of children, but it was a sensation and a box-office hit, because it was in Icelandic.

My father did not get along with my crazy friends, and they didn't get along with him either. It didn't help much when I told them about his future language. They interpreted this by saying that on the outside a blind chicken would sometimes find a grain of corn.

In their eyes my father was a pitiful and crushingly boring normal man. He was one of those who could not free himself from his straitjacket, one of those who thinks the way one expects them to. During all this I asked myself quite seriously, why they were so willing and ready to accept me. Did they perhaps see me as one of their own? In their eyes did I not belong to the normal ones?

When I was unsuccessful in selling my father to them as at least half crazy, I pursued another course of action, in the opposite direction. I presented him with two poems that in my opinion revealed the creative potential of my friends, and that I especially liked:

Þambara vambara þeysi sprettir
því eru hér svo margir kettir
Agara gagara yndis grænum
illt er að hafa þa marga á bænum

Heggur skalla í harðan skalla
Himbroðskallaviður
Otaði skalla ofan í skalla
Og í því skall hann niður.

A translation doesn't make much if any sense, since there is not much in the two quatrains. The first one it is about cats, and that one should not have too many of them on a farm. The second concerns bald heads that mightily crack against each other.

Surprisingly, my father seemed to be quite taken by this rather unusual poetic art. It surprised me all the more because I could not believe that he understood this piece of Icelandic lunacy. He told me that he could promise that in Germany and especially in Bavaria there were all kinds of gifted nonsense poets. He then gave me a few samples, none of which I understood, but they caused him to smile to himself.

It was no secret that my father wanted to make far-off Germany, and especially far-off Bavaria, more to my liking. I understood him, but that didn't mean that I had even a dream about settling there. I had my eyes set on my future, as an Icelandic writer. This is not uncommon among Icelanders as a professional goal, which is certainly related to their joy in playing with language and well-placed words.

My image of a Bavarian was of chubby men with clumsy-looking shoes and cut-off socks. These men wore formless stiff pants made of leather, *Lederhosen*, that were held up with matching suspenders. On their thickset heads they wore cone-shaped hats with an artist's brush in the headband. My father assured me that Bavarians spoke a language that was in its articulation superior to the hissing sounds of German. Furthermore, the Bavarian language was far more advanced than German. It could no longer continue to develop because they had foolishly written it down.

I remained firm; I wanted to live in Iceland, forever, and I also wanted my brother to stay so that everything remained as it was. My father could stay if he wanted to, was ready to fit in, and had taken on the customs of the land that he admired and honored. But especially he should stop requiring my mother to fry potatoes in hot grease and get used to boiled food. He loved pepper and that was like a thorn in the eye to us, but otherwise we got along with him.

CHAPTER EIGHT

In the Urban Jungle

Fall came, and everything was different from what I had imagined. My parents had agreed to separate us brothers: Gunnar was to go to elementary school in Germany, and I was to complete the elementary grades in Iceland and then transfer to a German high school, called a *Gymnasium.* I was well aware that people around me said crazy things, and that they told me they wanted to do crazy things; that was nothing new to me. I had gotten used to associating this with reality, or that they might sing a song like "Up, up and away to far-off lands," or something similar. When I did return in the fall from my grandparents, back to the civilization of Reykjavik, it was like being struck by lightning. My father had already disappeared with my little brother and returned to Germany.

The absolutely impossible assignment to steer my brother on a clearly safe path, with his uncontrollable need for freedom, had become for me a constant challenge. And now it was all gone. I thought back with nostalgia about the time when he nearly drove me crazy, with his daring and his apparent lack of sensitivity to cold, heat, pain, and all of the other things that drive normal people crazy. It was clear to me, his caretaker, so to speak, that he had gotten on my nerves, but at the same time he had been the driving force that pushed our common activities to that irrational point where stories arise.

I thought back about the frighteningly wonderful birthday surprise we had prepared for our mother. It was such a shock that its effect was felt for weeks thereafter.

For quite some time I had experimented with matches and matchboxes, and had learned from my classmates how to make little explosives with them. First you needed a hollow key, a nail that fit into the hollowed-out space, and then you tied both onto a string that you could wrap around your arm. The hollow space in the key was then filled with the substance scraped from the striking surface on a matchbox, and with several matches. Then the nail was put in and the string could be swung around in such a way that the nail would strike a stone or a wall. When it worked properly, the nail was driven into the hollowed out key and set off the explosive. If all went according to plan, the result was an ear-splitting bang.

In order to improve on the explosive effect, I tried to work out the right mixture of the scrapings from the striking surface of the matchbox. I did all of this in the kitchen of our little house. In the process I learned that I could make a wonderful salve from the material off the matchbox. In the dark it glowed, green and mysterious.

The two of us laid out a plan to prepare a special birthday surprise for our mother. I set about it right away by hoarding the striking surfaces until I had a veritable pile of them. I put the whole pile on a kitchen tray and lit it, thus acquiring a good quantity of the wonder-salve.

We got undressed and rubbed ourselves with the stuff, from head to foot, then stood in front of the floor lamp and waited until we heard our mother's footsteps. Just before she opened the door we turned off the lamp. Then we did an ecstatic dance in the smoke-filled darkness, like beings from another planet or shining up green straight from hell, howling loudly the whole time. Unfortunately I couldn't see the expression on our mother's face, but I heard her say: "For God's sake!" Considering the unusual situation, I didn't really know how to interpret her words. The surprise worked, but happiness was in short supply, especially when my mother learned about the chemical makeup of the salve that glowed so magically. The salve, like the smoke that filled the house, was enriched with green phosphorus. Under the best of circumstances, it could not have been unimportant for our health. The resulting compulsory bath reminded me of the pain inflicted on us during the children's boiling at Laugarnes. Whatever we had breathed in was our problem.

Even though this undertaking did not result the way we wanted it to, we did not feel bad, not even when our mother complained about the aftereffects. On the contrary, even the subsequent and degrading purification orgies remained in our memories as a glorious adventure, but not exactly an heroic deed.

On another occasion, my little brother went right along with me when we decided to greet visitors to the asylum at the entrance gate, in the spirit of the place, the *genius loci*. The gate had apparently stood open since the asylum was built, and had rusted in that position, thereby welcoming all guests. In order to keep the sheep grazing in the area from making use of this inviting opening, someone had dug out a low trench and covered it with iron pipes, like a cattle guard.

The pipes were laid wide enough apart that when sheep tried to cross the ditch, they would get their legs tangled up and would not be able to get all four legs on the pipes at the same time. They seem to have sensed this when they first saw the pipe grid and didn't even try to cross it.

At one spot they had made a mistake in placing the pipes, or in digging the ditch. The distance between the end of the pipes and the edge of the ditch was so large that skinny little kids could climb down through the opening. That's exactly what we did, and we had a lot of fun when the automobiles drove right over us.

As a result of having so much fun in the ditch, we got the idea to work out some kind of greeting ceremony. Since the white gate columns stood on the right and the left sides of the ditch, the cars always drove pretty much in the middle of the grid work. There was a rather wide area where the tires never touched, and so we decided to put our idea into action right there. We waited until we saw Ásbjörn's panel truck rapidly approaching in the distance and then climbed down into the grid-covered ditch. In doing so we could not see that the limousine of the head doctor was following the panel truck.

Just before Ásbjörn's truck reached the gate, we stuck our hands up through the grid work and waved them quickly back and forth. The effect was baffling, even though we could only hear what was happening, not see it. Ásbjörn slammed on the brakes in his truck and was thus able to turn out in a huge cloud of dust and dirt into the city bus turn-around directly in front of the gate. Our plan to get out of there in a hurry was complicated because the second car, the one with the head doctor and several very important government representatives, were surprised not just by the children's hands but also by the actions of the panel wagon. It flew over the iron guard and came to a stop a good distance beyond, also in a cloud of dust and dirt. We would have had enough time to flee, but we weren't sure whether more automobiles were coming. The excitement drowned out any other sounds from the road, so there was no other choice but to await our fate down in the ditch below the grid.

We heard a lot of loud cursing, mainly from Ásbjörn and someone who was riding in the panel truck with him. From the other side, we could hear more refined talk, and, to my astonishment, some laughing. When six faces looked down at us, we feared the worst, but the head doctor had decided to show the men and the one woman how professionally and nicely the mentally sick were treated, whether they understood or not. Ásbjörn took on the task of stopping traffic, at least the one car that followed, and was very pleased not to have to make any difficult educational decisions in front of the high-ranking officials standing there. Helgi, the head doctor, waited patiently until we had climbed out through the hole in the grid-work. He could see that we regretted something—even though it was simply that we had not seen the second car. Then he said in a calm, almost insignificant tone of voice, that he hadn't noticed that there was such a large gap in the grid.

He seemed to be interested only in the flaw to the grid, and did not utter a single death threat. The ganglia in my head were nevertheless rattling around. What was going on here; who was playing a prank here? Ásbjörn also seemed to understand the head doctor's tactics, and acted as if nothing had happened, only as if something was not right with the damned grid. All that day and for several days after that, I suffered more hellish pangs of conscience. Something terrible would be coming, I was sure of that. Some kind of punishing mechanism was about to be set in motion.

At one point, however, our paths did cross, and he looked at me, smiling in a most friendly way. He had always done this, maybe just not the same way, more like we shared in some secret. That's what I thought anyway, but maybe that's just what he wanted.

Playing pranks alone is not nearly as much fun as when there are two of you. My brother had always been with me for such nonsense, so I of course never thought that he could one day be far away in Germany. Even though it was unthinkable, my brother had in fact left us, and my interests moved more and more to what I could discover and do in the city, away from the asylum. I learned first of all that there was little to discover and nothing to do there without money. Up to this point in my life, money had played virtually no role. I had never even seen any money on my grandparent's farm, and in the insane asylum there wasn't anything to buy, thus no money there either. In the city it was quite different; here, everything was based on money. My classmates were always talking about it and the things they could buy with it. I began to think about the fact that they continually thought that way, then I thought about what I might be able to do with money, and finally how to get some of it. The latter seemed to me to be the most difficult.

It soon became obvious that you either got it from your parents, or you had to sell something to someone. This something, at least in the beginning, had to be acquired without money.

There were only a few things that could be sold among my peers, things of such value that they could be gained without having to pay money for them. There were some boys who dealt in fur remnants that they secretly took out of the furrier's garbage bins. I befriended one of them, and he told me where to look, and when I did I was caught, but thanks to my fleet-footedness I was able to get away through the butcher shop next door. Furriers, I soon learned, were very low in the city's food chain; they were actually hated by the other children—mostly boys—who roamed freely in the back allies. Among the intellectuals of the street children were those who dealt in film. I was irresistibly drawn to them.

Getting the goods always centered around garbage bins, primarily those behind movie houses. This has nothing, absolutely nothing to do with healthy nourishment, since the best they had at the movie house was just popcorn. But the name might have had something to do with biology. In good Icelandic, one speaks of *Kvikmyndahús,* which could be translated as "house of living pictures."

For some unexplainable reason, the camera operators in the movie houses were continually preoccupied with shortening the films they were showing. They cut out sometimes shorter and sometimes longer sections and threw them in the garbage bins, so that the audience saw less and less. It is thus not surprising that people preferred to see a film when it first arrived and was still new.

The film strips had developed into a regular commodity among the boys in the city. It was never a matter of how long the strips were or the number of pictures on it; it was about what was on it, the contents on the film.

Again, however, a distinction was made between the scenes and the actors. The most valuable were pictures where Johnny Weismüller could be seen playing Tarzan. Also of high value were pictures of Roy Rogers, his horse Trigger, Charlie Chaplin, and Buster Keaton, as well as various versions of Laurel and Hardy, especially when they could both be seen from the front, and finally the Marx Brothers.

Pictures with female film stars were much lower on the scale, down there with landscapes and film credits. You could trade the pictures, but you could also sell them. The customers were primarily boys from better-off families who did not want to pick around in the movie house garbage bins. Girls were also buyers, but difficult customers to deal with, and we, the boys, had to cater to their strange tastes. I was better at understanding their mind-set, simply because I lived at Kleppur, where I had different experiences from the other boys.

So I had an advantage in this business. I bought relatively cheap images of female film stars from my competitors, like Jean Harlow, Mae West, Mary Pickford, and Marlene Dietrich, then sold them for a profit to young girls interested in them. Unfortunately I didn't know too many of them, and so I soon had to look around for a new business opportunity. The hottest items on the market were napkins that all the girls wanted, but most of all it was chewing gum.

At the time chewing gum, especially the products of the Wrigley company, were an unattainable pleasure for normal citizens of Reykjavik. Money didn't make a big difference since officially chewing gum was sold exclusively to taxi drivers. It was thought that chewing gum was a proven means of helping tired taxi drivers not fall asleep.

This time I didn't even try making deals; I turned immediately to the promise of recycling, that no one yet controlled as far as I knew. The chewing gum market was not limited to fresh wares—they were difficult to come by—but, rather, used gum in various stages of preservation. This depended primarily on how carefully and professionally the former owner had treated his gum. The biggest sin of all was to spoil the chewing gum with foodstuff such as bread crumbs. Any subsequent attempt to separate them out merely led to unsatisfactory results.

The recycling process had two goals: the original taste and the original shape. This required appropriate packaging, so that it looked just like a new product. For several weeks I conducted a whole series of experiments in our little kitchen. The most important additives were peppermint flavored toothpaste and sugar.

I tried pickling, boiling, kneading, and layering, but success was extremely modest and didn't lead to a flourishing business.

Lækjatorg, Main Square with city buses

Finally I gave up on these experiments since they made our house unbearably smelly. Next I took up a halfway regulated but extremely low-paying job as a newspaper hawker. Daily newspapers were the most important employers of boys my age, but the money earned through street sales of newspapers was hard-earned.

The competition was fierce, and the winter weather created enormous problems when I tried to carry out my work, like getting into town and picking up the papers from the publisher. It is difficult to hand out newspapers and to grasp the coins with mittens on, so cold fingers were a necessary part of the profession.

The main place for hawking papers was the Lækjatorg, which means Brook Plaza, a square in the middle of Old Town, where the bus lines from all around the city come together. People got on and off here, and purchased newspapers so they could read them on the bus or at their workplace. Dozens of young boys stood there, large bags filled with newspapers hanging from their necks. Some were my age, but most were a little older. Only one of them was clearly much older; we called him *Óli blaðasali* (Óli the newspaper seller). Óli was something like the uncrowned king of newspaper sales. He was the only one with a covered spot to sell his papers, directly at the entrance to the city druggist. Among the weather-beaten boys out on the open square, there was a rumor that his amazing health and weather resistance came from the healing and medicine-laden air that streamed out of the drug store and into his workplace. He could never really get sick because he breathed in all of that medicine with every breath. Óli sometimes behaved a little strangely, especially when someone tried to move in on his favorite selling place. This happened only every once in a while, and by an innocent beginner in the business of selling newspapers. Óli's special status came from the fact that he didn't have to shout, like normal paperboys did, to sell his wares. We young occasional sellers all screeched, shouted, or sang the same melody and the same text: *Morgunblaðið, Alþy'ðublaðið, Þjóðviljinn, Vísir* (Morning Paper, Peoples Paper, National Will, Pointer), chanting the last one with the name *Tíminn* (Time). Actually it was of no real significance what we shouted out, since everyone knew that we were selling newspapers and there were no other papers in Reykjavik than these. Even those boys who were too lazy to pick up all four papers from the publishers sang the same song. Any other one would not have fit the melody.

The first time I got off the bus at Lækjatorg, I was impressed by the earsplitting cacophony of the newspaper boys' wailing, and I thought it might be more pleasing if they all sang together, in unison, with one voice. Even then it seemed strange to me that they didn't stop or lower their shouting when they stood directly in front of a customer and handed over a paper; they continued to sing loudly, directly into his face.

Later, when I became one of the newspaper sellers, I tried to do away with the silliness of this bad habit, and after a while I was able to convince some of my colleagues to sing in chorus. We earned several looks of astonishment, but there was no noticeable boost in sales, so we soon stopped with our attempts to sell more papers through singing.

At just about this time, Reykjavik got its first traffic light. It became necessary because a real traffic jam developed several times on one of the main streets, Laugavegur (Bath Street), and by simple multiplication it was easy to see what would happen in the future. Among the newspaper boys, this led to heated discussions about whether the area where cars stopped for the red light would be the best place to hawk our papers. The decision was left up to the local guru, Óli. When he made no move to abandon his spot in front of the drug store, it was clear to the rest of us that the traffic light was at best a second choice.

By taking up newspaper sales, I had advanced beyond bartering in the back allies. Now I had actual money: real paper money. I kept the first bills at home in an album, where I also kept the pictures from the movie house garbage bins. I even thought about making the money bills more beautiful with colored pens so that I could then exchange them for other bills. When our neighbor, Head Nurse Guðríður, caught sight of my first products, she didn't act as though she was inspired. Instead of being enthusiastic or happy, she looked serious and informed me that the bills did not belong to me but to the government. It was difficult for me to understand that, since I had earned that money through hard work. I had raised the value of the bills by making them more beautiful, and the government should be happy and thankful! Then when I heard about threatening punishment, which I really couldn't comprehend; I decided for safety's sake not to expand on this business opportunity.

I did, however, stay with images and turned to stamp collecting, loved by everybody in Iceland. Money could be exchanged on the Lækjargata for postage stamps. To my astonishment, the head nurse had nothing against making the stamps more beautiful, but she told me that they no longer had the same value after they had been colored. I kept secret the exchange of colored stamps that I had already done.

Earning money is one thing, spending it another, and both must be learned. I exchanged the boring money bills for more interesting postage stamps, little pieces of paper for little pieces of paper. I didn't know what else to do with the money I had earned. Were the stamps worth the drudgery? I often asked myself this, especially when the weather was bad. The question became more pressing when the stamps got more expensive, those I thought I had to buy because they were missing from my collection.

If I could soon find a better way to spend my money, then I could give up the tiring work on the Lækjatorg. I couldn't spend all my money at the movies, first because the films weren't exchanged often enough, and second, most of the films were not for children under twelve years of age. There was also the possibility of spending money in a new fast-food sausage stand on the Lækjatorg, but this short-term cash flow solution didn't impress me.

Along with chewing gum, lemonade proved to be a highly marketable commodity. Coca-Cola and orange soda were the most desirable, but they were for the most part unavailable. The same was the case for what one still today calls *Öl*, or *Maltöl*. This "malt extract" is prescribed for strengthening mothers convalescing after childbirth.

Among the boys in the city who were dealing with the cost problem, a custom arose which led to questions of another kind, those of a cultural nature. Some smart aleck came up with the idea that with lemonade it was really just a matter of taste; the drink itself could be replaced with water. Several boys at a time could share one bottle, using it like a kind of mouthwash. In this way the contents were never subjected to reduction. I thought a long time about such behavior, but never came up with a convincing answer. Perhaps, I finally thought, the taste was finally just used up, but I felt little desire to firm up my suspicion through applied experiments.

Then one beautiful summer day, I discovered the wonderful world of Tivoli. Here were a number of interesting possibilities to address the spending side of my cash flow. Tivoli was at that time the amusement park for the citizens of Reykjavik, inspired by the grandiose model in Copenhagen. If you didn't know any better, you might think of Tivoli as an open-air version of Kleppur. In Tivoli people spent their good and hard-earned money to be tossed around in circles, horizontally and vertically, or forced into tiny little automobiles to repeat all of the accidents they had just luckily escaped in city traffic. In the hall of mirrors you could see just how awful you could appear, and in a glass labyrinth you could get just as lost as in the worst office building in town.

In a remote section of the park, there was an unimposing barrack where great deeds awaited little heroes who had money in their pockets. It was a kind of play hell for children and childish adults. Various games were lined up along the walls, all of which had one thing in common: a slot to put money into. By doing this, the machines went into action, and there was then one or two minutes to accomplish some great task. With a little steam shovel, you could try to pick up the prime target, a wristwatch, from a pile of small junky prizes. You could try to dislodge an avalanche of coins, or, by pressing hard, and with some difficulty, on two boxing-glove-like handles you could view pictures of a woman who removed more and more of her clothes. This last game was reserved for grown-ups and very strong men. We little runts had no chance of getting to see anything, even when we concentrated our efforts, like acrobats. Fascinating rumors about the apparatus made the rounds among us, but no one seemed to know what the final scene in the striptease actually looked like.

For many of the games, the reward was merely a number flashing somewhere, and when the number was high enough, a bell rang. There was also a game with a little car that had to be steered along a curvy road painted on a revolving tin plate. And then there were weapons to shoot at strange animals, and much, much more.

In Tivoli there were also shows that drew us boys into their spell.

Tivoli amusement park

At the top of the list was the appearance of the strongest Icelander, and every one of the boys claimed to be related to him. Actually this was true, since all Icelanders are more or less distantly related to each other.

Everyone placed great value in knowing their relatives and their acquaintances, and the relatives of the acquaintances, and so on. When my mother talked with her relatives or acquaintances, it sounded like they were each reading from a telephone book. It helps a lot on such occasions that Icelanders, with few exceptions, do not have family names. Instead they have the name of their father, and if this is not sufficient to distinguish among the numerous Jóns, who are the sons of a Jón, then the grandfather's name is added on, who probably was also named Jón.

The strongest Icelander was named Gunnar Salomsson, and, according to the comforting words of my mother, was related to me. The muscleman, however, lived mostly abroad, where he was called Ursus (Bear). His appearances were most impressive, especially for children my age. He could tear thick books in two, length- or crosswise. Anyone who could do the same was promised twenty-five thousand Kroner. He lifted two horses with their riders, an elephant, and a fully filled car off the ground. He smashed stones with his bare hands and twisted iron bars into unusual shapes. Six of the strongest men in the audience tried to choke him with a rope, but to no avail, of course. Ursus was indeed a model to emulate. Every boy wanted to be like that! The image was clouded a little when he got into a street fight with a Danish Greco-Roman wrestler and came up short. Finally he had to call for help from the police.

From the very beginning, selling newspapers lacked the excitement of competition. You could get along; with a lot of effort you could even earn a little pocket money, but you had to simply give up on any ambition of earning more than the others by trying harder. There was no career ladder to climb, unless you wanted to compete with Óli, but no one came up with this senseless thought, probably out of respect.

The only chance to get ahead as a child was offered by the annual campaign for donations to the Red Cross. Right after the war, everybody knew about the beneficent effects of this organization and was prepared to contribute a few Kroners for their work. Whoever collected the most was honored as *Sölukongur* (sales king), and subsequently introduced as such. Because I always got up early and had already worked out a sales strategy, I garnered the title for two years, and received a children's book each time as my prize. In the third year, my competition declared war on me. Children of wealthy parents, I learned, were going to be supported through massive contributions by their parents, and thus would be helped to win. My only trump card was Kleppur; more precisely, the inmates of the asylum who were always eager to give away their money. I just had to find a way to keep my competition from going there while I was away. If I could keep them out, after the big competition in town, I had a strong winning hand in my suit.

Three of my unconstrained friends among the patients were only too happy to help me out in such a noble undertaking. Their only task was to make themselves look frightening and cut off my competition at the entrance gate—better still, on the road in.

Just what they did on the day in question remained unknown to me and out of my control. Because of my business activities in town, I could not get away. Just before the end of the collecting activity, I went back to Kleppur to cash in, and I could soon see that the inmates had done their work. I was even scared and frightened when I met them at the gate. They had blackened their faces and hands with soot and wore old shredded bedclothes on their heads that hung down over their shoulders, like a wild hairdo. When they saw me coming up, and before they recognized me, they jumped out from behind the gate columns, snarling and screaming, spread their fingers like attacking wildcats, and ran toward me. When they recognized and greeted me, they seemed very proud of their actions. According to their accounts, they had chased off a whole bunch of children, and even some suspicious-looking adults. That could have resulted in an amusing postlude, I thought, but I simply praised my happy friends for their accomplishments.

I was lucky, since knowledge of the activity at the gate had not yet spread among the personnel at Kleppur. My namesake, the head doctor, was the only one who had a direct view of the entrance gate, but he didn't appear to have noticed anything, or else he didn't get involved because of some complicated therapeutic issues on his mind, I surmised. I was never quite sure, with him. In any case, I thought the worst was yet to come and would concern me only if one of the adults who was scared away complained to the asylum directorship. By then I would have long since been crowned *Sölukóngur*, and no one could take that away, since it was for such a good cause as the Red Cross, and for the third time! I would for sure be forgiven my rather unusual collecting strategy and once again be seen as a great hero.

The next day came and nothing happened; really, nothing at all. I was not called to the asylum director's office, nor was an announcement made in the local newspaper. The head doctor, however, had this subtle smile on his face. I could only wait and hope. A week passed and when nothing happened, my fear gradually changed into anger. Something was being done on the quiet behind my back, and there was something odd about this business. Only a telephone call to the Red Cross could clarify the matter.

Telephone calls in Iceland were without cost at that time, and there were telephones in the halls of the asylum, for use by anyone. This led of course to amusing misuse, which then led to fees being charged. The call to the Red Cross was soon accomplished, but with no results; they didn't yet know, they said, who would be the king of collecting. They also didn't know when they would know. So I called every day and asked if it had finally been decided.

The many telephone calls must have finally got on somebody's nerves. My mother was called by the Red Cross and received something like a peace offering. Indeed I was once again the king, but they didn't want to make this generally known so as not to demoralize other children during the next collection campaign. They were ready, however, to present me with a fitting gift, if I would promise not to participate next year.

First and last prize

The gift was to be presented to me personally by the famous cathedral provost, Séra Jón Auðuns, but would not be made public. There was no talk about my dark wheeling and dealing and the dubious donation tricks. My heart and to some degree my conscience were relieved, and I of course agreed. Victory was mine, even if it turned out to be my last one.

In the following years, they changed the procedure so that the children received a percentage of the collection as their prize. That wouldn't have interested me anyway.

The deeper I moved into the urban jungle, the more questionable it became whether that was what I really wanted. On the one hand, I felt drawn to life in the city, even sucked in, but at the same time repulsed by it. It became progressively more difficult to maintain my outsider status and to use it to my advantage. Nobody was impressed by my being an outsider; for most of them, I was an Icelander with a funny name. My residence at Kleppur seemed to be more impressive, at least to the children my age.

A difficult problem developed out of where I lived. Kleppur lies on the east side of Reykjavik, a little outside of town, but nevertheless on the eastern side. Landakotskolí, the Catholic school, lies in the middle of the western part of the city, and war reigned between youth gangs in the west and the east. It was a pretty serious war, and it sometimes called for action by the police and rescue teams. It became more and more difficult for me to stay out of this activity. Neutral mediators or similar intermediaries were never in question. Anyone who didn't participate was soon suspected of being a traitor and could no longer feel secure. That all seemed quite well known, and I didn't feel the slightest urge to participate in the nonsense, but I was a commuter across the frontier and on school days moved back and forth between the fronts.

Street battle of the dwarfs

In the east and in the west there were no secret unions; all were known: in the east, and thus responsible for me, was the group called *Tígrisklóin* (Tiger Claw), and in the west their fervent enemy was the organization *Sannir Vesturbæingar* (True Westerners). The war consisted mostly of small skirmishes, but occasionally it would take on the characteristics of a battle carried out with all the elements of a real war. In the beginning, the weapons were relatively harmless and consisted of wooden cudgels, clubs, cooking-pot helmets, and stones. This was soon to change, however, following the logic of war and intellectual progress; the swords were fashioned out of iron bars, and in place of the cudgels there were now spears and bows. The stones were fired with rubber slingshots, and new weapons were soon created, using bicycle chains and nail-studded flails. Subgroups were formed with threatening names like Bloody Skulls, Night Owls, Sharp Noses, and Snakes. A kind of secret language was developed, and soon there were impressive initiation rituals consisting mostly of rather disgusting and painful tests of bravery.

Partisan battles and sabotage were especially favored. Sometimes an outhouse was turned over, and sometimes an inattentive opponent got a cow pie in the face. In later years most pleasurable was throwing spoiled oranges and rotten eggs as projectiles into the middle of a gathering of the opponents. More direct attacks consisted of poking someone with a needle, and, as the ultimate use for chewing gum, sticking it into someone's hair. Such guerilla actions were often the prelude to an organized battle in which several hundred boys faced their opponents in well-thought-out battle formations.

The battle continued with loud howling and screaming until one of the warriors was seriously wounded or started bleeding profusely. With that the battle was over; the group with the wounded warrior lost, and we went home until the next time.

The police were quite powerless in controlling us. There were no ringleaders, no time plan, and only a few rules. It was sufficient if two or three boys, fired up by the devil or whatever, but mostly by the mobilization of the opponents, ran around the streets and let out loud war cries. No one wanted to stand back like a coward or a traitor.

There was a constant state of war between the parts of the city, but the reasons were just as many as they were unexplainable. There needn't be a particular cause for the war activities, just renewed or clear continuation of earlier reasons to fight. Just when and why this utter mischief got started was not known by anyone, and it was also not clear just how to end these horrible episodes.

My fate in this warring depended absolutely on my diplomatic abilities. I went to a school in enemy territory, there was no doubt about this; but I was not a stranger, more the friendly enemy from next door. I was more like a competitor in a rather unfriendly sport battle.

At school my classmates consisted for the most part of girls, who, like women worldwide, distanced themselves from the war battles, or had to suffer from them. The relatively few boys in my school belonged for the most part to that bourgeois type that found it unnecessary to seek their luck in street battles.

Diplomacy meant in particular to relativize friend and enemy, to be a little bit friend and a little bit enemy. It was just enough that I could not be completely allied with either side, and was thus removed from the two-class system. Especially, however, it was important to appear harmless and unsuspicious. This is easiest to accomplish if one has the reputation of being somewhat strange in the head, or as we say in German, lightly *meschugge,* off one's rocker. I had no problems with that.

On the other hand, it was not easy for me to stay out of the battle action. Something very mighty rose up in me. I was not happy at all when I thought about what was going on in the city, and what pleasure it would be for me to go into battle, side by side with committed comrades, laying into an adversary bravely defending himself. Maybe I could even become a ringleader and then bathe in the warmth of amazement by my fellow warriors! Then I could show off my wounds as trophies or bring plundered goods home, like valuable wheels from children's wagons to build soapbox carts with.

Reason, however, finally won out, and I continued to cultivate the status of a harmless, intellectually lightly confused boy unfit for war activities. Nevertheless, I wasn't spared. It happened on a day when there were still classes in the afternoon, and I had tried to keep the peace by getting away as fast as possible on the bus. I wasn't successful this time, and I found myself surrounded by a horde of True Western members who then blocked my path in a most provocative way.

I didn't know them, they didn't know me, but that was enough. My senses were precisely between war and peace, rising anger and comforting reason. One of them then spit in my face, and I lost my cool. Just what happened, the details, cannot be reconstructed, but this much is clear: two opponents lay on the ground and I found myself fleeing. I ran as quickly as I could in the direction of Lækjatorg, with a whole pack of infuriated True Westerners on my heels, carrying sticks and cudgels. Right when I ran past the entrance to the Salvation Army building, disaster caught up with me. Running as fast as I could, I turned around to see where my persecutors were, and that is when I didn't see the steps leading into the Salvation Army and fell flat on my face. I picked myself up immediately, spit something out, and continued to run until I felt more secure sitting in the bus. What I spit out were two teeth, at least large pieces of them. When I greeted my mother with a large smile, she let out one of those light cries so seldom heard from her. What I had gained for my bravery in battle appeared to her a horrible disfiguration of my face. I offered to go back and look for the pieces of my teeth that I had spit out, but that did not calm her one bit.

If I had known what I had done to myself, my joy about the little victory over the True Westerners would have been far less clear. Polishing down of the tooth remnants to little points, in order to put artificial crowns on them, took two days, hurt a lot, was smelly, and constantly overburdened the ancient polishing drill. I found the new teeth far more beautiful than the old ones, however; they were much whiter, so much so that the old ones looked older. I proudly told everyone who asked how I, in such a heroic way, came to possess these new teeth. For a boy between ten and eleven years of age, his appearance in the mirror doesn't play such a large role. In general, one also does not do much to look better for the parents—bathing was enough. Even my haircut was not chosen for aesthetics, only for practical and hygienic reasons. Most practical is the butch cut, and this was thus often chosen. Actually, one small cosmetic compromise was the little bunch of hair left at the front that stuck out from the plain wool cap and looked a little like a ponytail.

More troublesome, I felt, was the single freckle that appeared one day right in the middle of my nose. I tried to figure out what it would look like if this was the beginning of a freckles invasion.

One freckle

When the one and only one stayed, I was concerned about why it was right in the middle of my face. This mark on my face did not escape the attention of the other children, and I was in danger of becoming the subject of their superstition. And so I made up one story after another to explain the annoying freckle on my nose. None were very believable, but I was still astonished at how ready my classmates were to accept my explanation. Sometimes I was just on the verge of believing my own fairytales and thus had to find my way back to the truth by making up a new lie. That was almost like being at home, in the insane asylum, or so I thought—but only almost.

CHAPTER NINE

The School of Better People

Better people are probably found everywhere, just like better horses, cows, and sheep; worse also. The Protestant minister believed that, as did the Catholic priest, but my mother didn't think that way; at least, I don't think she did. Just like me, she didn't believe that better people were to be found in the Catholic school, in Landakot. She sent me to this distant special school so that we had our peace with my Bavarian relatives, who were concerned with the salvation of my soul. It was bad enough, they must have thought, that their poor child was supposed to grow up in an insane asylum, with crazies of every sort; but then among Protestants—that clearly went too far!

It meant, for me, that I had to take a long bus ride every day, from final stop to final stop. On good winter days, I could make this a little more sporting by doing what all my peers did, *Taken* (*teika*—hang on to cars).

It was a kind of sport just on the other side of legal. Today we call this ski sport *Jöring* (slipstreaming), but then we were without a horse and without skis. Instead there was the omnibus or an automobile, and those rubber shoes already described.

The art in this sport consisted of hanging on to the bumper of a car, unnoticed by the driver, and being pulled through the snow- and ice-covered streets. Omnibuses were particularly good because they always stopped at marked bus stops, and because the driver could not see what was going on behind his vehicle. As a rule, the driver also did not want to get out at every stop and check the rear end of his bus. If he did, however, as soon as he had chased the sportsmen away, by the time he had squeezed behind the steering wheel again they had gotten back on their contraptions. There was always the danger, at less slippery places, that we might lose our grip on the bus and be run over by cars following behind the bus. The car drivers also knew about our game, and for safety's sake they kept their distance. Even more elegant than rubber shoe-sledding was an expansion of this sport by using a *Skíðasleði* (ski sled).

Ski sled

This sport contraption was not a sled traveling on skis, as the name might suggest, but rather a sled on flat, raised strips of iron, more like ice skates. Other than that, there was little relationship to real skis. The ski sled would better be described as a chair mounted on skids, and on the back of the chair there was a handlebar, much like on a child's stroller. The driver held on firmly, kept one foot on the runner, and shoved the sled forward with the other one, similar to riding on a scooter. A passenger sat on the seat, or you could place baggage on it. When sliding along, the boy sitting down was responsible for holding on to the bus.

During that time the *Skíðasleði* was something like an automobile for the little ones of Reykjavik. The streets were neither cleared of snow, nor salted, just driven over until they were packed down, and thus became an ideal trail for a few sleds.

Sledding on hills, the favored type of sport today for sleds, was not suitable for this means of transportation. Virtually no one had a sled for that kind of fun. Here you needed creativity, and once again we chose automobile inner tubes—the universal material in those days—or whatever else we could find, like our school backpacks, or just the seat of our pants.

No matter what, every trip finally ended at the Landakot school where they finally got accustomed to my unbelievable home address of "Kleppur." My German family name seemed to be a fitting addition. A half outsider has more problems to master than a full outsider, since the latter can at some point become accustomed to being different. I was sometimes an insider and sometimes an outsider, a native and a foreigner, on occasion accepted and, at other times, the cause of misunderstanding, suspicion, and trouble. Dipping my feet into alternately hot and then cold water could not be avoided, not even when I was absolutely prepared to fit in. Actually this was the way I was anyway, and so I set out to cultivate the status of someone who cannot be easily labeled. It brought me respect, but at the same time a kind of friendly distance from my classmates. It was easier for them not to include me in all of their doings, but at the same time they placed value in telling me about all their heroic deeds—or at least what they thought were heroic. Sometimes it made me mad not to participate in the glorious and great undertakings of my class comrades, but at other times

I was really happy not to have been a part of one escapade or another.

My comrades were, for the most part, extremely happy about their rude punishment of the lower strata among us. Soon they got tired of teasing and punishing us, and began to feel that physical education was just too burdensome. They next set their goal on getting out of the afternoon drudgery. They succeeded in getting doctors' certificates documenting orthopedic handicaps of various kinds. The school principal didn't notice that an ophthalmologist, one of the boys' fathers, issued all the certificates. (Icelandic orthography, like orthopedics, was certainly not one of the strong points of the Dutchman.) The ostensibly handicapped nevertheless had to take swimming lessons, since swimming is, for Icelanders, almost as important as reading and writing, and for this there was no medical dispensation.

I would have liked the physical education instruction if it hadn't always been on Friday, if I hadn't always been invited to lunch in the city by the family of a famous piano maker, and if there hadn't always been half spoiled ray fish to eat at their place. I could smell the stinking fish when I was still one whole block from the family's house, and I had to resist the natural instinct to flee as fast as possible. At some point the smell of ray fish began became associated in my head with sports and for a long time ruined my pleasure in physical education.

Carpentry in the tower

My school friends didn't have to deal with such problems; they simply had better things to do in the afternoon. This didn't apply to every kind of afternoon instruction. Guðrún's legend hour was never missed, and the "carpenter's hour" by Sister Klemma, up in the school tower, had also especially enthralled them. Heaven knows why. Those hours were in many ways like an adventure, since the nimble Klemma was never able to stay in one spot for very long. She just disappeared sometimes for a short time, sometimes for longer, and sometimes she just forgot that up in the little tower room extremely unreliable Viking ancestors had been left to their own doings.

About halfway up the small and creaking wooden stairway to the tower room, where the instruction was conducted, we went past an unusual workplace where plaster figures were made. The producer of these little figures was a man named Ferdinand, called Ferdinand the Bellringer. At some time in the past he had been the one to ring the tower bell, but now he had to be satisfied with a little school handbell. Ferdinand was a little eerie, rather small and stocky, and wore a beard that made him look like God, or like a mysterious dwarf from one of the old Icelandic sagas had fathered him. To compensate for the loss of his role as the primary bell ringer, he had begun a new kind of activity in the tower: making little religious and secular plaster figures.

Ferdinand

Sales were always difficult, and once when I stole a look into his attic work studio, I saw absolute armies of white figurines on the floor and all lined up in columns on shelves. There were whole sections devoted to Madonnas, Christ figures, and dogs and cats, all in different sizes and in various poses.

Ferdinand, who was always rather laconic, instinctively saw in me someone like himself, an outsider. I was probably the only student who talked to him about his plaster figures, and who praised him for his products and his artistic ability. Visibly moved, he gave me a plaster cat, one which I kept for more than a half century.

Klemma's instruction in woodwork consisted of making one single object, a rather heavily built but very stable shelf that was to be given by the student to his mother at the end of the school year. This proved to be a very clever pedagogical move, since it was not only a matter of the grade Klemma gave out, but also of the honor one could acquire at home and the advantages that accrued from this gift.

Final product with my mother's initials

Because of the tower guard's long absences, my class comrades were inspired to think about heroic deeds that could be carried out from up there. Particularly amazing, in their opinion, would be to get past Klemma and smuggle *Öl* into the tower. In Scandinavia, *Öl* is primarily understood to be beer, but in Iceland it is also that alcohol-free malt drink that is prescribed for nursing mothers. Real beer was certainly brewed in Iceland, but only foreigners consumed it. Icelanders were strictly forbidden to imbibe beer. Please note that these restrictions were not for religious reasons—since alcohol was sold and drunk in every other way, preferably as schnapps—but were for construction workers, who on the work sites always had a bottle of beer in their hands. Sooner or later someone would get drunk and then a tool, probably a hammer, would fall from his hand and land on the head of an innocent passerby. It was believed that such horrible falling hammers must be avoided at all costs. One of the boys in my class had a great relationship with the local beer and *Öl* producers. I have to believe that he had been initiated into the plan for our unique heroic deed. The rest of the story must be seen as part of the Icelandic heroic legendry, since I learned about the course of events only from oral tradition.

A decisive prerequisite for the daring plan was a trapdoor in the tower roof that was apparently used at one point to heave the bell into place, and, if needed, to take it down again. For the participants, it was unknown if the hatch could even be opened so that from there, a rope could be lowered to raise a case of *Öl* up into the tower room. A reconnaissance team took on the task of slipping past Ferdinand and his plaster army in order to see whether the trapdoor could even be opened. They chose a particularly stormy day so that the creaking of the stairway would be covered up by the general creaking of the roof trusses.

Everything seemed to be going according to plan: the team got into the school building without being seen, and then got past Ferdinand unheard, and up into the tower. They set about opening the hatch in the roof right away, but they were not really overburdened in their task— more like under-burdened, because they overestimated the task's difficulty. The hatch cover didn't just open up all by itself, but scarcely had they unscrewed it when a strong gust of wind seized it, and it flew off in the direction of the church. According to the boys on the team, it flew back and forth, rolled over like a stunt airplane, and then landed quite hard out in the meadow, right in front of the semi-Gothic church.

The approximate flight path

The storm blew right into the pale faces of the troops peering out of the tower, since during its flight there was nothing they could do to control where the large piece would land—or, better said, crash. There were several sensitive structures in the trapdoor hatch's path. Diplomatic complications would have resulted if it had landed on the property or indeed the building that housed the Russian embassy. The Russian embassy was clearly the nearest building in that wind direction. Maybe, so we later thought, we might have been able to count on a little understanding on the part of the Russians, since they were the main consumers of the outstanding Icelandic beer, Egill Skallagrímsson. Thank God it never came to this kind of diplomatic discussion. Ferdinand was frightened by the loud noise up on the roof and was able to see the final stage of the flight manœuver. He then headed off the fleeing storm troopers and, with soft and only half-understood mumbling, helped them carry the hatch cover back up to the roof and screw it down. He didn't ask how this event had come about—he was and is a wise man—and so the legend of the flying trapdoor came to a happy end.

I was never really sure if I should believe the story. The most unbelievable stories are often truthful, and the most believable are made up, or are simply lies. Sometimes it is the case that it doesn't really matter if the legend is true or not; what matters is that it pleases.

The clever boys in my class offered unbelievable truths in large measure. Gradually I also gained the impression that they really liked telling me about their activities, but I was not—and am still not—really sure just why. Maybe they saw something in me like a specialist for what was humanly unusual, for a polished expert who moved among the more or less dangerous inmates at the insane asylum, the one who knew exactly what was going on. In any case, I could imagine that the stories were true, but I couldn't stop being amazed and astonished at the actions of these brave comrades.

High up on their list was anything that was forbidden, especially gambling. Gambling for money was likewise of high value for the street children, to whom I also belonged. Highest in popularity was *Fimmaurahark* (pitching pennies), which could be loosely translated as a five-cent riot. To carry out this fuss, two parallel lines were drawn on the ground, several meters apart. The competitors took up position behind one of the lines and took turns tossing five-cent coins as close as possible toward the other line. The winner was the one who came so close to the line that the opponent would give up. The coins still on the ground were then picked up and tossed up in the air all at one time. While they were still in the air, the victor would call out heads or tails, and then he got all of the coins that corresponded to his call. Games of this type among my schoolmates couldn't even evoke a tired, sympathetic smile. They played poker for sums of money that were not made known, but rumors abounded. The poker games always took place where the parents were known to be away, the players' arrivals taking place in cars of other parents. Cars were quietly and softly pushed out of the garage and then, some distance away they were started. The underage boys themselves did the driving, but sometimes older boys with driver's licenses were employed as chauffeurs. They were especially proud of their nocturnal driving skills, and it was always admirable to cruise around in one of those heavy American limousines, unrecognized by the police. Such daring undertakings required some preparations, like a thick pillow to sit on and an imposing fatherly hat on. It was still common back then to drive a car with a hat on one's head.

The stories they told me sounded more like dreams than the actual truth. They could see that in me and decided to give me a lesson. One beautiful evening the doorbell rang at our house, something quite unusual for us. My mother opened the door and found herself right in the middle of a group of midget-like figures dressed as Chicago gangsters. In front of her stood three eleven-year-olds with oversized hats pulled down deep on their faces; outside was a large black limousine, and they asked to speak to me. My mother, who was naturally used to dealing with such crazy situations, had difficulty maintaining control. She didn't know the boys, who claimed to be my friends from the city. It had always been difficult for her to criticize the actions and behavior of others, even when it was a matter of uninvited guests.

She called for me, and I appeared in front of my classmates in my pajamas. Much to my surprise, they looked at me impassively and then, polite and friendly, they invited me to take a spin with them. I was almost as astonished as my mother, and was also very polite and friendly when I thanked them for the offer and said that they should have asked me earlier—that I had already gone to bed and did not want to get dressed again.

My comments seemed to be acceptable to the mini-gangsters; they just wished us a nice evening, got back in the black limousine, and drove off spinning their tires. My mother could scarcely conceal her confusion about this nocturnal happening and thought about calling the police. She wanted to know if I actually knew the boys; I most likely said yes, but once again not really very clearly. She thought about it again and then obviously gave up on her plan. Probably she didn't want to get someone in trouble with such a vague suspicion. Who knows—maybe she even enjoyed this crazy scene.

Later she repeatedly pointed out that it hadn't been easy for her to determine the real age of these pint-sized crooks. Besides, they behaved very politely and discretely.

To be sure, even if they were well educated, the boys could not stop bragging at school about their nightly adventures. Actually nobody believed them—other than me, of course—but these stories left marks on their reputations, and in the final analysis, stories were told about them that were far below their station in life, and finally got them in real trouble.

One unusually beautiful morning there was a strange turmoil at school. The students were strictly and personally forbidden by director Ubagh to go out onto the playground during recess. Rumors circulated, and all seemed to revolve around harmful pictures that someone had painted on the walls of the school. These rumors were confirmed when Ferdinand, armed with bucket and brush, hurried past the school window and got to work on the wall, which we of course could not see from inside. We surmised that it must be a real and very nasty image.

After school we saw the shoddy effort from the street, since Ferdinand's scrubbing was not all that successful. It was a larger-than-life simplified drawing of a naked woman. More precisely, it was two curvy lines for the left and the right sides of the body, a long y-shaped stem and two O's with a point in each one. That, then, was the evil that they wanted to protect us from at all costs! For me the image suggested the power of art and the way one could present something.

My classmates were of course immediately under suspicion for this graphic misdeed, but they were honestly indignant and rejected any attempt to blame it on them. I would have been the first to be accused for this crazy action, but in the meantime I had gained the reputation of a model student, and besides, I was Catholic and had recently received my first communion.

The riddle of its origin was never solved, and the artwork proved to be quite indelible. The children got used to it, and no one seemed to suffer any noticeable damages. Finally the artwork was removed from the building by scraping down the stucco, all the way down to the supporting wall, but up to this point it seemed to have become some kind of symbol of the worldly openness of the Catholic educational system.

Even though I had pushed it as far back in my mind as I could, I still was saddened that soon my world was about to change most dramatically. I would have to leave all my friends, schoolmates, and even the cherished images of my enemies. No one other than my mother would speak my language, and not even the Danish I had learned would be of any use to me.

I was of course curious about this new and supposedly wonderful world, but I couldn't imagine leaving Iceland and Kleppur for several years, perhaps even forever.

Wouldn't that mean leaving myself behind and becoming someone else, someone that I didn't really want to be? Someone who perhaps didn't want to be an Icelander living in a crazy house? I decided to do the only thing that I could—to wait out the course of events and only then to think about it.

CHAPTER TEN

The Strange Homeland

When you know that everything will be gone tomorrow, then you can enjoy today twice as much.

First, school was just over when I became aware that there were also girls sitting in the classroom. Not just a couple of them, but actually the majority. Up until this point, I had thought of them as nothing more than empty chairs in the room. The girls always planned parties to celebrate the end of the year, but for me these were not going-away parties since I actually didn't know any of these girls personally.

In a kind of strange and (up until now) unknown way I began to regret this when it was already too late and I had lost sight of these young women. Now I had to keep my head above water in the whirlwind, and move away from my old and trusted world and on to a new and eerie path.

For once, and for the first time in my life, it seemed that the days became shorter and the events came thick and fast. If I accepted the fact that it was a parting for an unknown period of time, I had a lot to do. If, however, I pretended that I would be gone only for a short time and would soon return, then I could almost just get away with saying "see you soon." The latter possibility was more pleasing to me, and so I just ignored our departure as long as I possibly could.

Because everything had to go as fast as possible, but not just for that reason, we decided to take an airplane. It was of no importance that I had not done well on the ocean voyage, that I had to suffer through those bad days on the high seas, but out in the fresh breeze.

The flight was indeed much shorter, but I had the impression that the sickness of a several-days sea voyage was concentrated down to the time of this trip. The four-engine plane, called a Skymaster, took us on an eight-hour roller-coaster ride and delivered us, not in our best condition, in Copenhagen. The flight was a hellish experience: being trapped in a flying machine filled with infirm, choking, screaming, and green-faced people. It was a world without the steady and healing forces of gravity. It was not a good beginning, especially for this new phase of my life—at least that is what went through my aching head.

In Copenhagen, the torturous trip was continued without pause, this time by train. It was a fast train, my mother told me. We sat for one whole day and one whole night squeezed into a small train compartment. Everything had a strong and bad smell to it, including me. To satisfy our hunger, we could purchase sustenance, or something similar, through the train windows when we stopped for longer periods at damaged train stations. On the station platforms, little rattling carts moved about with things to drink and something to eat. Hundreds of arms reached out of the train windows toward the vendors. I quietly decided to run away as soon as I could from this strange, gray, and unfriendly world and return to Iceland.

Our housing affected the Icelander in me as close and provisional, but then there was this wonderful weather and the lake for swimming, the garden full of fruit, and my little brother! There was much to discover. People acted hectic and resigned at the same time, tense and lackadaisical, in a word (or few) troubled, off balance, and mostly unhappy. Everyone seemed to be so busy and wanted to accomplish something very important.

Everybody looked hypnotized and stared straight ahead, toward what they thought would be a better future. There was planning, comparisons, and work!

My father worked the most, scarcely finding time to eat and sleep. He didn't bring in much money, but that didn't stop him from working like a crazy man. It's called idealism! What he did was of little interest to me, but I knew that it had something to do with language, and with several variants of the German language.

I didn't think about mastering his language; I just wanted to go back to Iceland as quickly as possible and become an Icelandic writer. Nevertheless, I learned German.

They all worked hard to help me. My grandmother especially took the time, and I worked with her because of my good manners, but it wasn't hard for me, anyway.

The German language seemed to be something like a dried-out wooden branch of Icelandic. But wood, I had to admit, is better for building than soft and living greenery. German spoke to my understanding, Icelandic to my heart. I decided to call German my father tongue and to keep Iceland accordingly as my mother tongue. It is not at all difficult to see that the two languages are related to each other. Thus I understood German in an unusually intuitive way from the very first day.

Later I tried to explain to myself my interest in etymology and the development of languages, and finally, in language in general. But in the end, I learned of the danger that comes from language—that it not only supports our thinking, but also limits it.

I didn't have a lot of time during this period for thinking, since no one left much time for themselves or for others. The trademark of German family life was, then as now, my religious education. There was a clear and insistent suspicion that in Iceland, Protestant or even heathen thinking had infected me, and so they thought about fast and effective help. In their eyes there was one quick solution. In her young years, my aunt had been a member of a religiously strict Catholic youth organization called the *Quickborner* (living spring). These *Quickborner* were still around, and they put on an annual and strict youth camp near the *Wieskirche* (meadow church) in Steingaden. The organizers were ready to participate in the reeducation of a Catholic youth religiously screwed up by Vikings, and before I knew what was happening I found myself, still somewhat speechless and somewhere far away from Diessen, in a group of about a hundred boys my age.

During the day there were early and late prayers, but at night we fought. There were two long church services during the day, and two long religious lessons taught in the forest, but thank God I did not understand them. The nights were more pleasing to me and seemed more in the spirit of paramilitary youth organizations. Every night a wild struggle ensued, but it was always well planned out. There were two sides: the attackers and the defenders. One group had a red wool ribbon on the right wrist; the others, a blue ribbon on the left wrist. The defenders had "castles" up on hills; the attackers gathered in trenches in front of them. A police whistle gave the starting signal, and war began. At the end of battle, whoever had the most wool ribbons, taken as trophies from the enemy, won and was declared the warrior hero of the day. The wounded received medical help, and then everybody went to bed.

There is a special story about this. The sleeping quarters were on the third floor of a huge hay barn, up in the loft section, and consisted of a narrow five-meter wraparound gallery. Old stamped-down (or, rather, slept-down) hay was spread on the floor; enough, according to the leaders of the camp, to keep the young people from going soft. *Safety measures* was at that time still some kind of foreign phrase, much like *fire safety*. We climbed up to our resting places on a wobbly ladder by the light of two or three storm lanterns. On the ground floor, the farmer had his hay-drying machine, pitchforks, and various other iron implements, about eight meters below the sleeping balcony—with no rails, of course. One might easily imagine what kind of unpleasant results a fall from this balcony into the machines parked below might have had. The children would thus be careful, so the headmasters apparently thought, but the teachers' quarters were much more secure and comfortable, off in an inn used in the past by pilgrims. In fact, one night one of our group, probably a sleepwalker, fell off the balcony and onto the prongs of a hay rake. It didn't serve as a horrible example, however, since he climbed virtually unharmed back up onto the balcony. If we hadn't heard him dragging around, we wouldn't have known anything about the incident.

I was so relieved when I was allowed to return home that I was ready to accept any imaginable religious nonsense if they would just let me stay away from instruction of this kind. In that way, one can say that my reeducation was completely successful.

Scarcely back home, I found other teaching on the schedule; namely, school. I was to present myself for entrance tests at the Secondary Modern School and Gymnasium in Weilheim. My chances of acceptance were not the best, since my intuitively learned German up to this point was insufficient for school. The first try was painless, but it was extremely frustrating for my father, who had accompanied me. The director, a small man with a big cigar in his mouth, apparently confused Iceland with Estonia, and couldn't be corrected. He rejected us with the assertion that he had only had bad experience with Estonians. With no success, we took the narrow-gauge train back to Diessen. My father fell into grumbling, and I saw my chances for returning to Reykjavik increasing.

A few days later my father found an article in the newspaper that the aforementioned director had been removed from office as a result of his past political activities.

We set out once again, straight back to the school in Weilheim, where a new wind was blowing. An American, Mister Verminghouse, who had no real knowledge of German, took over temporary leadership of the school, and was most pleased about the new student with just as little language knowledge as he had. But still there was the prescribed entrance exam, and so I had to take it.

It was not at all clear to me why my father was so confident that I would pass the test, especially since I didn't give myself any chance at all. I could understand the international language of mathematics most of all, or so I thought, but there was one thing he hadn't thought about. They gave me word problems, and my father was not allowed to translate them for me, even though he protested vehemently. The German essay fell flat from the very beginning, but they still let me sit there for three quarters of an hour thinking about my empty page. Nobody was interested in my knowledge of Danish, and my English sounded to the examiners a little too foreign. Finally, when the religion teacher showed up and wanted to hear me quote the Apostles' Creed, my father lost his patience—and he knew something about mistreatment. He protested, and they then agreed that I could say the creed in Icelandic, and for this they were willing to give me a note of "satisfactory" for my effort. They could afford that much, since I had already failed resoundingly.

As a result of this unfair examination, everything was spinning around in my head, and I couldn't remember the creed at all. My father looked at me with anticipation, and in my heart I knew I couldn't embarrass him with my memory loss. They don't understand me anyway, I thought, so it really doesn't matter what I say. I knew enough Icelandic poems, and so I began to recite one:

Ólafur reið með björgum fram
villir hann stillir hann
hitti fyrir sér álfa rann
þar rauður loginn brann
Þar kom út ein álfamær
gulli snúið var hennar hár
Velkominn Ólafur liljurós
Gakk í björg og bú með oss
Ekki vil é með álfum búa
Heldur vil ég á Krist minn trúa
Bíddu mín um litla stund
meðan ég geng í grænan lund
gekk hún sig til arkar
gekk upp saxið snarpa
Ekki muntu svo héðan fara
að þú gerir oss kossin spara
Ólafur laut um söðulboba
kyssti hann frú með hálfum huga

The religion teacher, a stocky man with a mouth like Sylvester Stallone, looked at me from the side and in a strange way, and I could see him trying to say the creed at the same rhythm in German. My father didn't turn a hair, which I interpreted to mean he understood what I was doing. Apparently he did the same thing as the examiner, and when I reached the place with the kiss, he nodded quite obviously, and I interpreted this to be an indication that I should end my declamation.

The instructor clearly had serious doubts that my presentation could have been the Catholic creed in Icelandic. He of course had no proof. The two men exchanged their views, but I didn't understand them. Then my father asked me in Icelandic if I could say a Mary-prayer in Icelandic by heart. I couldn't do that, but since I had already told one tall tale, I could continue with that. So I presented them with the last stanza:

> *Vendi ég mínu kvæði í kross*
> *villir hann stillir hann*
> *Sankti Maria sé með oss*
> *Þar rauði loginn brann.*
> *Amen*

The doubts by the religion teacher remained—or were actually even stronger than before—but my father still didn't let on, and finally they agreed to give me a grade of satisfactory, even if it was only to temper justice with mercy.

The whole examination was a farce, and everyone who participated in it knew that. Rector Verminghouse had apparently previously decided to give me a chance, in the form of a one-year period of grace in German language instruction. In the final analysis, that was enough.

Now my presence as a student was tolerated, and in the high school that my father had praised so highly. I had my doubts, and they weren't lessened when I learned that the school had been founded by a crazy man, a Bavarian king who ate his breakfast when his fellow countrymen were eating their evening meal, and who liked to paddle around in a swan-shaped boat on a man-made subterranean lake. He later committed suicide. I decided to accept my fate for the present with dignity and composure. It soon turned out that I had taken on a lot.

The school really didn't have anything regal about it. Instruction took place in two shifts, and not just in classrooms but also in barracks, and even down in the coal cellar. The teachers themselves were heavily marked by war; many were wounded and patched back together. Others lost their nerves during the war and then paid honor to the school founder by taking their own lives. Still others remained intellectually stuck in war or prewar mentality. The latter thought of me as a young Aryan warrior from the far north, and so one day in history class I had to demonstrate the bodily advantages of the Germanic race. Germanic, I soon learned, meant that a German warrior knew how to fight bravely, with a spear. An especially well-developed lower arm worked to a warrior's advantage. Non-Germanic, on the other hand, was presented in the figure of a small, dark-haired, curly-headed boy who was placed next to me. This figure did not have these special traits and thus did not qualify as a superman. It was all very awkward for me, but I didn't realize until it was too late what was going on. The words needed to protest were lacking, anyway.

Even physical education was still filled with reminiscences of past war experiences. The motto for presentations could have been "hard, but with heart." "Line up by size and count off." I soon learned what kind of voice to use when counting off; it sounded like dogs barking. Physical exercise followed the counting off, like a drill on a casern parade ground. Run, duck, throw, crawl, and then do it all over again, again, and again. At the end, as a reward, we did battle with a medicine ball; or, when the weather was good outside, with a handball on the cinder court. When the weather was bad, the cinders stuck to the ball, and when you were hit, it cut into the skin on your underarm. No one came up with the idea to complain, so I also kept quiet and just wiped the blood off on my pants.

We played basketball in the winter in the gymnasium. I wouldn't have had anything to complain about if the baskets had not been positioned directly over the gigantic iron stoves used to heat the gym. All things considered, physical education was not very good at developing enthusiasm for sports.

In other classes it was similarly strange. The art instructor was especially thin-skinned and threw inkwells at unruly students. The math instructor couldn't count, which was no wonder, since his actual profession was opera singer. In the war he had lost his voice and was quickly retrained in mathematics and physics. He suffered here too, because he had a phobia of electricity, also brought on by the war. When he was in a really good mood he let us chose an opera concert to play and then gave us a quiz. The German instructor had all kinds of tubes around his stomach, to take care of his intestines, and seldom talked about anything else.

What kind of insane asylum had I landed in here! If I had only been able to stay in Kleppur! I worked it out, learned the language, made friends, but I still remained a foreigner, at least in my mind, just like my mother. The more I acquired German culture, the more I became a neither-nor, neither Icelander nor German. I felt it painfully, that I had to choose a new and personal place for myself. My father may have noticed this, and regretted it, but he also found himself between two posts—teaching positions, to be exact.

Someone who is uncompromising is seen as hardheaded by some and steadfast by others. Anyone who alters his convictions is always more popular and acceptable than someone who knows what he should be convinced of.

Seekers and doubters are never valued, not in any system. They are hated, they are angry, they are extremely unreliable and bothersome; but without such people everything comes to a standstill. They are both the seat of unrest and a source of life combined.

In my thoughts I have never left Kleppur, my crazy Icelandic home, a Kleppur that hasn't been the same for a long time now, that exists only in my memory. The crazy people at Kleppur had become my friends; I belonged to their family, to their everyday life, and they belonged to mine. They didn't send any letters to me in Germany, but they were nevertheless a part of my life here; they live on in my thoughts. I have much to thank them for, and hope that my presence and attention gave them some pleasure and helped them bear their fate.

Without them I would not have become what I am, intellectually; without them, many doors would have been closed to me.

I learned an important lesson in Kleppur: all are crazy in their own way, and we are all crazy together. Everybody is crazy; the only question is: too much or too little?

May we all move in spirit from one mistake to the next one; at least we can move, develop, and try, and that means affirming the hope in whatever we are facing. That's what is important—I think.

Made in the USA
Monee, IL
07 July 2026